E S T A T E   P U B L I C A T I O N S

TAUNTON

BRIDGWATER

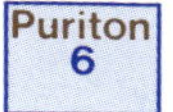

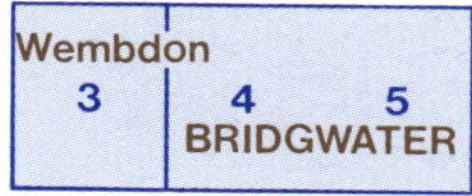

North 6
Petherton

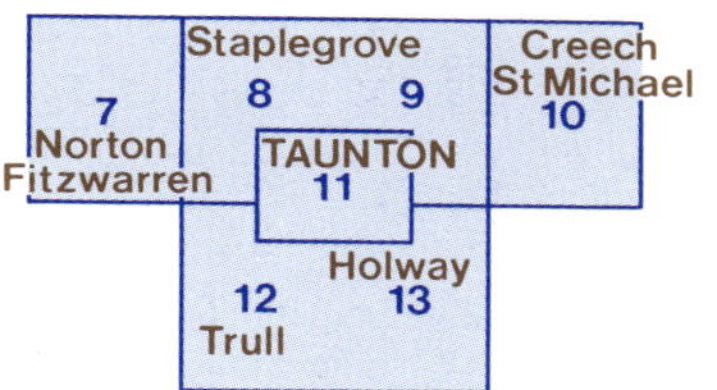

ROAD MAP	page 2
TAUNTON ENLARGED CENTRE	page 11
STREET INDEX	page 14–16

Every effort has been made to verify the accuracy of information in this book but the publishers cannot accept responsibility for expense or loss caused by an error or omission. Information that will be of assistance to the user of the maps will be welcomed.

The representation on these maps of a road, track or path is no evidence of the existence of a right of way.

Car Park	P
Public Convenience	C
Place of Worship	✚
One-way Street	→
Pedestrianized	
Post Office	●

Scale of street plans 4 inches to 1 mile
Unless otherwise stated

Street plans prepared and published by ESTATE PUBLICATIONS, Bridewell House, TENTERDEN, KENT.
The Publishers acknowledge the co-operation of the local authorities of towns represented in this atlas.

Ordnance Survey® This product includes mapping data licensed from Ordnance Survey® with the permission of the Controller of Her Majesty's Stationery Office.

ISBN 1 84192 174 2

2 ROAD MAP

A
B
C
D
1
2
3
4
5
6
Bridgwater
Bay
Burnham
on-Sea
Edithmead
B3139
Highbridge
Stert
Flats
Stolford
Huntspill
Steart
Stretcholt
A38
6
Pawlett
23
Puriton
Dunball
M5
Chilton
Trinity
A39
Lilstock
Shurton
Stockland
Bristol
Burton
Kilton
East
Quantoxhead
Kilve
Stringston
Stogursey
Combwich
A39
West
Quantoxhead
Williton
Holford
A39
QUANTOCK
Bicknoller
A358
Nether
Stowey
Fiddington
Cannington
18
A39
Charlinch
Spaxton
Wembdon
4
Stogumber
Crowcombe
Quantock
Forest
HILLS
Four
Forks
Durleigh
Lwr.
Aisholt
Flaxpool
Lwr. Vexford
BRIDGWATER
West
Bagborough
Courtway
Goathurst
24
Huntworth
Willett
B3224
North Petherton
Tolland
Ralph
Lydeard
St. Lawrence
Cothelstone
Broomfield
A38
4
Northmoor
Green
Nth.
Newton
Combe
Florey
East Combe
Cushuish
Thurloxton
Tarr
Langley
Marsh
Ash Priors
Bishop's
Lydeard
Kingston
St. Mary
W.
Monkton
Lyng
B3188
Fulford
Hedging
A358
A361
Fitzhead
Halse
Cheddon
Fitzpaine
Durston
VALE OF TAUNTON DEANE
Norton
Fitzwarren
Staplegrove
Monkton
Heathfield
A361
3
A38
4
Milverton
B3227
7
Heathfield
Knapp
Nth.
Curry
Oake
Hillfarance
Creech
St. Michael
Bathealton
TAUNTON
25
Ruishton
A358
Thornfalcon
B3187
Langford
Budville
Nynehead
A38
8
Bradford
on Tone
Trull
Stoke
St. Mary
8
Wrantage
Runnington
Wellington
West
Buckland
B3170
Orchard
Portman
W. Hatch
26
7
M5
SC
Hatch
Beauchamp
Holywell
Lake
Pitminster
Corfe
Beercrocombe
A38
Angersleigh
Blagdon
Hill
Staple
Fitzpaine
Sampford
Arundel
Wrangway
Ford Street
14
Bickenhall
Ilto
Luxham
Resr.
Staple
Hill
Curland
Ashill
Nicholashayne
Clayhidon
Windmill
Hill
BLACK DOWN HILLS
Rosemary
Lane
Churchstanton
Broadway
Fyfett
Horton
Culmstock
B3391
Stapley
B3170
Buckland
St. Mary
A303
Donyatt
Hemyock
Churchingford
Bishopswood

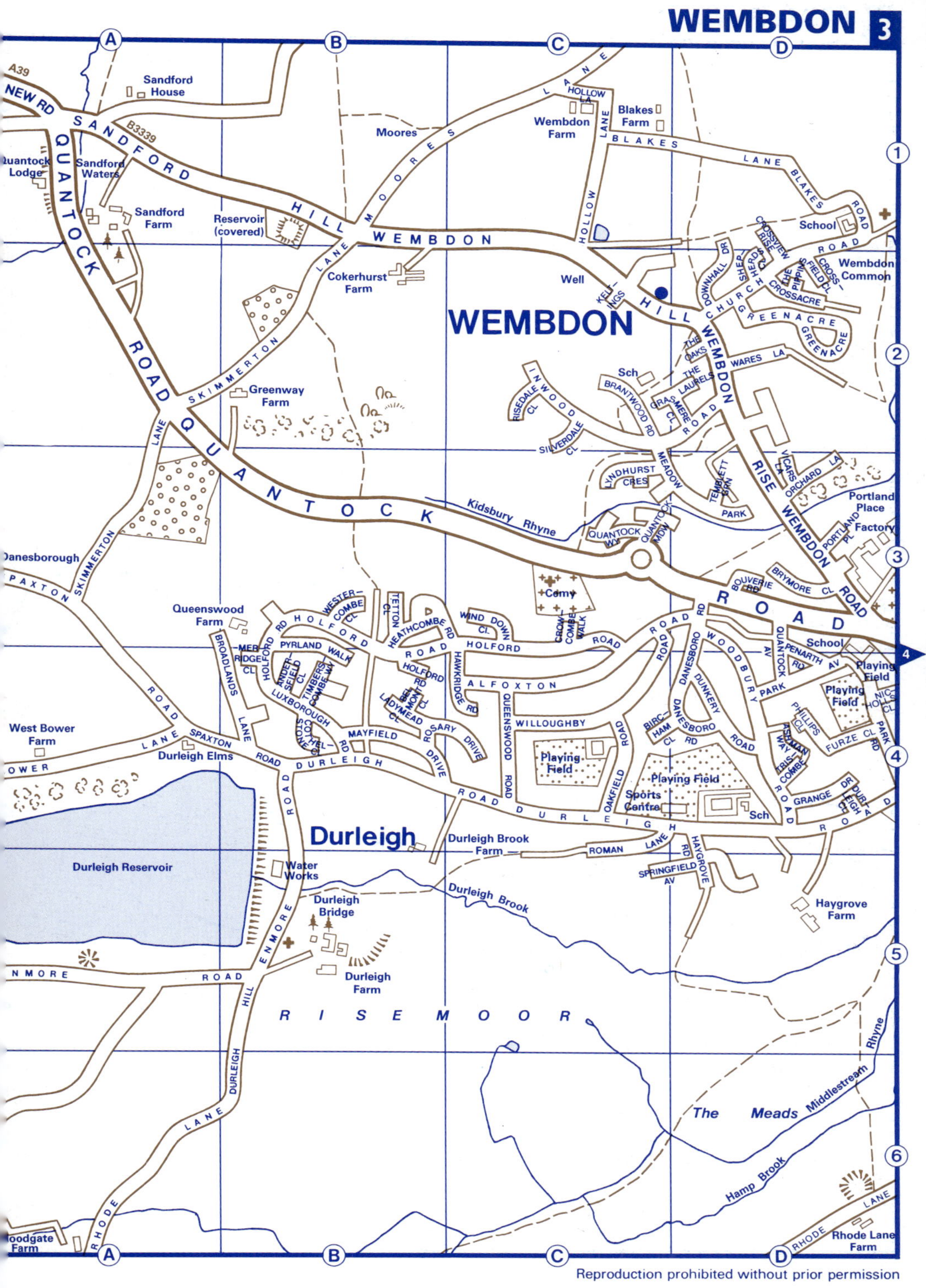
WEMBDON
Durleigh
Durleigh Reservoir
RISEMOOR
The Meads
Sandford House
Sandford Waters
Sandford Farm
Quantock Lodge
Moores
Reservoir (covered)
Cokerhurst Farm
Wembdon Farm
Blakes Farm
School
Wembdon Common
Well
Greenway Farm
Sch
Kidsbury Rhyne
Cemy
Portland Place
Factory
Danesborough
Queenswood Farm
School
Playing Field
Playing Field
Playing Field
Playing Field
Sports Centre
Sch
West Bower Farm
Durleigh Elms
Durleigh Brook Farm
Water Works
Durleigh Bridge
Durleigh Brook
Durleigh Farm
Haygrove Farm
Middlestream Rhyne
Hamp Brook
Rhode Lane Farm
Woodgate Farm
NEW RD
A39
B3339
SANDFORD HILL
QUANTOCK ROAD
MOORES LANE
HOLLOW LA
HOLLOW LANE
BLAKES LANE
BLAKES ROAD
WEMBDON HILL
SKIMMERTON LANE
KELLINGS
CHURCH ROAD
CROSSACRE
GREENACRE
WARES LA
WEMBDON RISE
WEMBDON ROAD
DURLEIGH ROAD
HOLFORD ROAD
ALFOXTON ROAD
QUEENSWOOD ROAD
WILLOUGHBY ROAD
WOODBURY PARK
PARK
SPAXTON ROAD
BROADLANDS LANE
BOWER LANE
ENMORE ROAD
ENMORE HILL
DURLEIGH LANE
RHODE LANE
ROMAN LANE
HAYGROVE RD
SPRINGFIELD AV
MAYFIELD RD
ROSARY DRIVE
PYRLAND WALK
LUXBOROUGH RD
WESTERCOMBE CL
TETTON CL
HEATHCOMBE RD
WIND DOWN CL
CROWCOMBE WALK
HAWKRIDGE RD
DANESBORO RD
DUNKERY ROAD
BIRCHAM CL
OAKFIELD ROAD
GRANGE DR
FURZE CL
PHILLIPS CL
ASHMAN WAY
TRISCOMBE
PENARTH AV
QUANTOCK AV
NICHOLLS CL
BOUVERIE RD
BRYMORE CL
PORTLAND PL
QUANTOCK WY
QUANTOCK MDW
LYNDHURST CRES
MEADOW ROAD
TEMBLETT GRN
VICARS LA
ORCHARD LA
SILVERDALE CL
RISEDALE CL
INWOOD ROAD
BRANTWOOD RD
GRASMERE CL
THE LAURELS
THE OAKS
DOWNHALL DR
SHEPHERDS CL
CROSSVIEW RISE
THE PIPPINS
CROSSFIELD CL
ANDERSFIELD CL
TIMBERSCOMBE WY
BELMONT CL
LADYMEAD CL
COTHELSTONE CL
MERRIDGE CL
DURLEIGH CL
DURLEIGH RD
A B C D
1 2 3 4 5 6

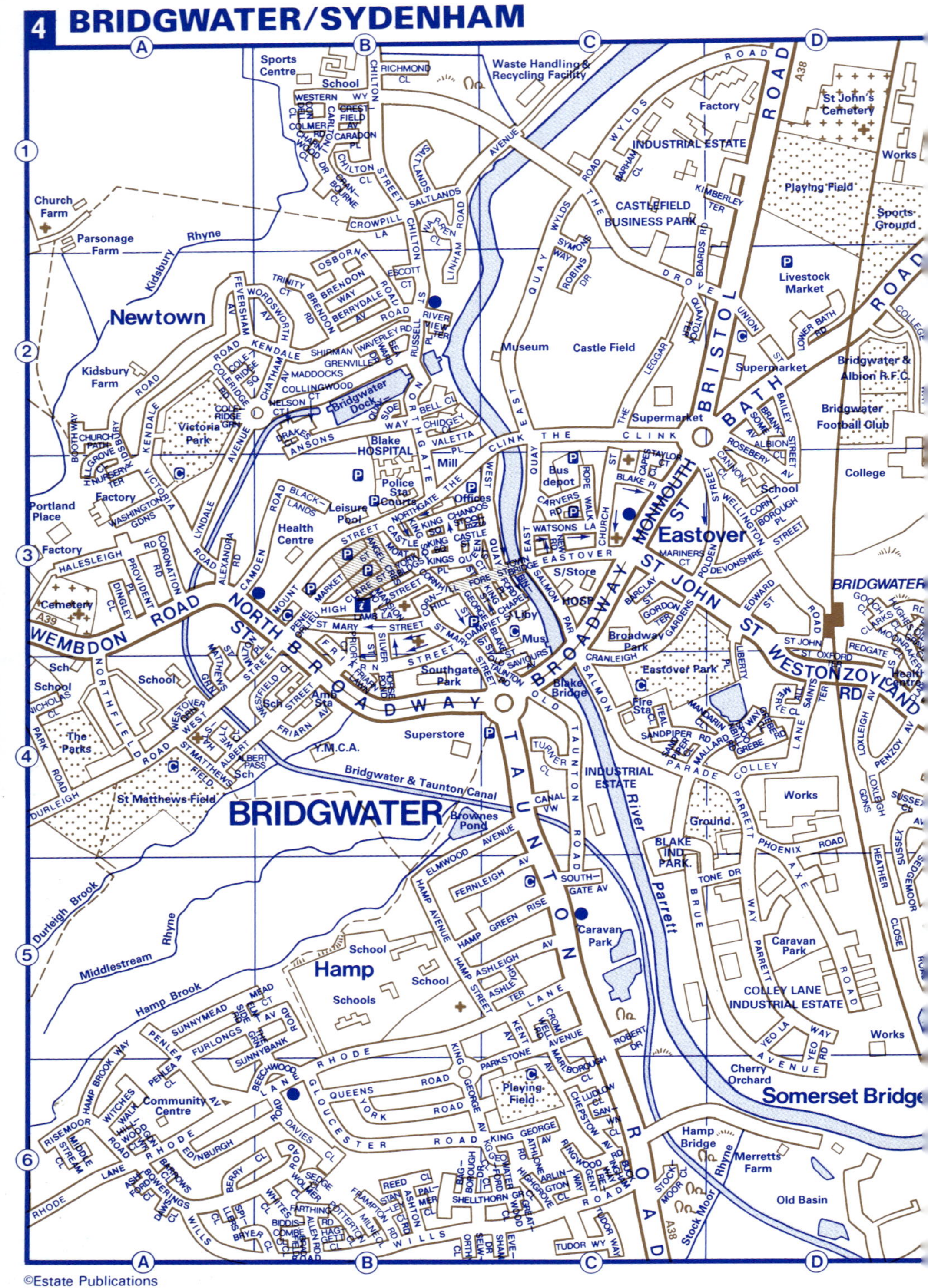
A
B
C
D
1
2
3
4
5
6
Sports Centre
School
Richmond Cl
Waste Handling & Recycling Facility
Factory
Industrial Estate
St John's Cemetery
Works
Playing Field
Sports Ground
Church Farm
Parsonage Farm
Rhyne
Kidsbury
Castlefield Business Park
Livestock Market
Newtown
Kidsbury Farm
Museum
Castle Field
Supermarket
Bridgwater & Albion R.F.C.
Bridgwater Dock
Bridgwater Football Club
Victoria Park
Blake Hospital
Mill
The Clink
College
Portland Place
Factory
Police Sta
Courts
Offices
Bus depot
Leisure Pool
Health Centre
Eastover
Cemetery
Wembdon Road
North Broadway
St John Street
Monmouth St
Bristol Road
Bath Road
Broadway
S/Store
Hosp
Liby
Mus
Broadway Park
Eastover Park
Bridgwater
Westonzoyland Rd
Sch
School
The Parks
Southgate Park
Blake Bridge
Fire Sta
Amb Sta
Superstore
Y.M.C.A.
St Matthews Field
Bridgwater & Taunton Canal
Industrial Estate
Works
BRIDGWATER
Brownes Pond
Ground
Blake Ind Park
River Parrett
Taunton Road
Durleigh Brook
Middlestream
Rhyne
Caravan Park
Caravan Park
Hamp
School
School
Schools
Hamp Brook
Colley Lane Industrial Estate
Works
Cherry Orchard
Somerset Bridge
Community Centre
Playing Field
Hamp Bridge
Merretts Farm
Old Basin
Stock Moor
Rhyne
A38
A39

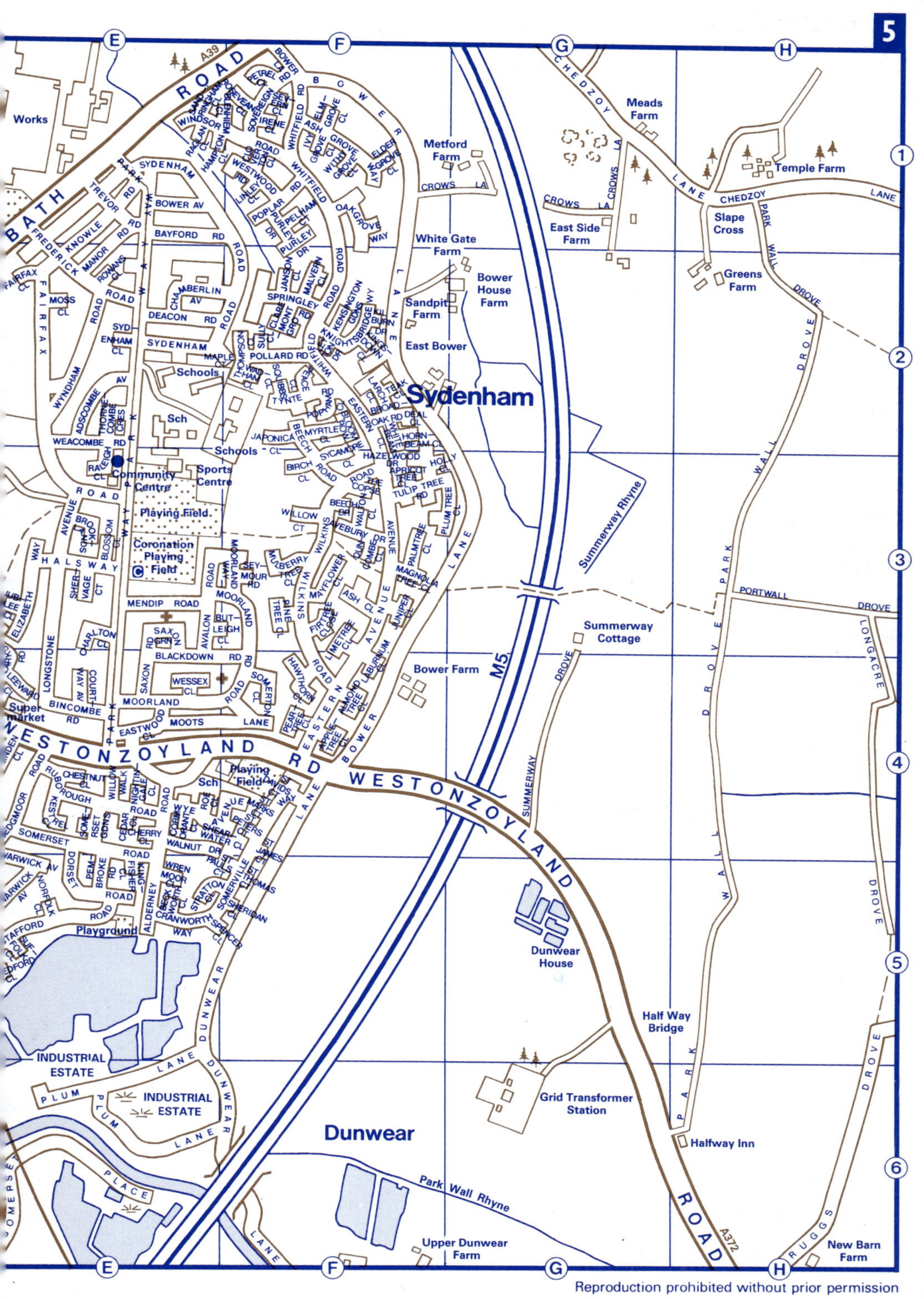
Works
BATH ROAD
A39
Sydenham
Metford Farm
Meads Farm
Temple Farm
Slape Cross
Greens Farm
East Side Farm
White Gate Farm
Bower House Farm
Sandpit Farm
East Bower
CHEDZOY LANE
CROWS LA
PARK WALL DROVE
Schools
Sch
Community Centre
Sports Centre
Playing Field
Coronation Playing Field
Summerway Rhyne
PORTWALL DROVE
LONGACRE DROVE
Summerway Cottage
Bower Farm
M5
WESTONZOYLAND RD
WESTONZOYLAND ROAD
SUMMERWAY DROVE
Super market
Playground
INDUSTRIAL ESTATE
PLUM LANE
DUNWEAR LANE
Dunwear House
Half Way Bridge
Grid Transformer Station
Halfway Inn
Dunwear
Park Wall Rhyne
Upper Dunwear Farm
A372
RUGGS DROVE
New Barn Farm

PURITON

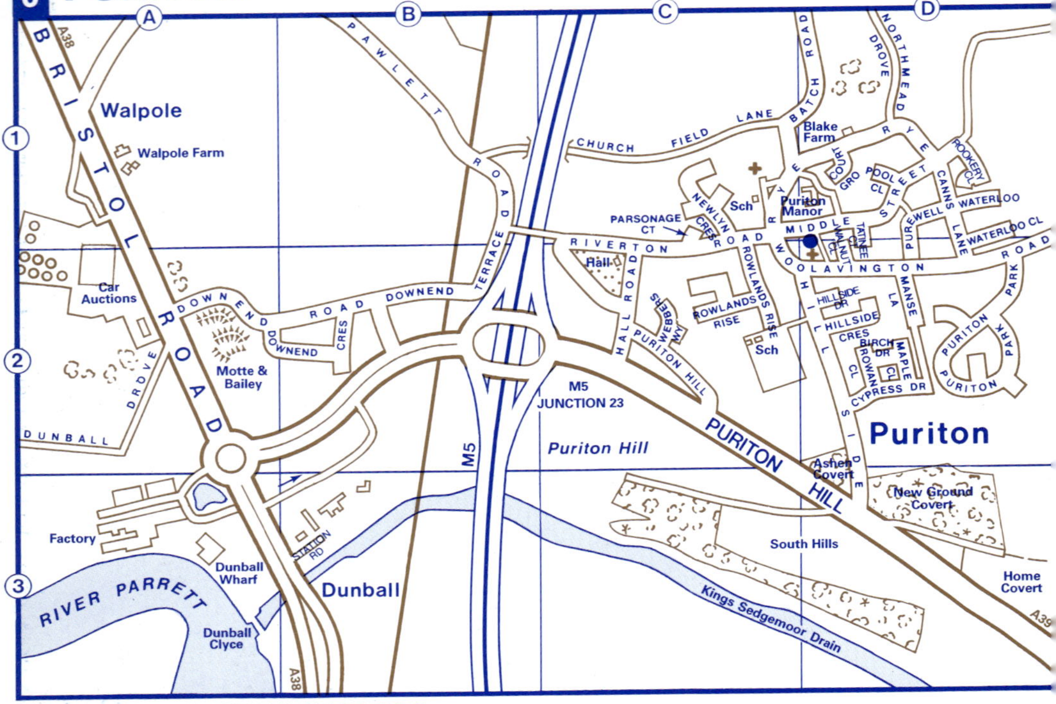

Walpole
Walpole Farm
Car Auctions
Motte & Bailey
Factory
Dunball Wharf
Dunball Clyce
Dunball
River Parrett
M5 Junction 23
Puriton Hill
Puriton
Blake Farm
Puriton Manor
Ashen Covert
New Ground Covert
South Hills
Home Covert
Kings Sedgemoor Drain

NORTH PETHERTON

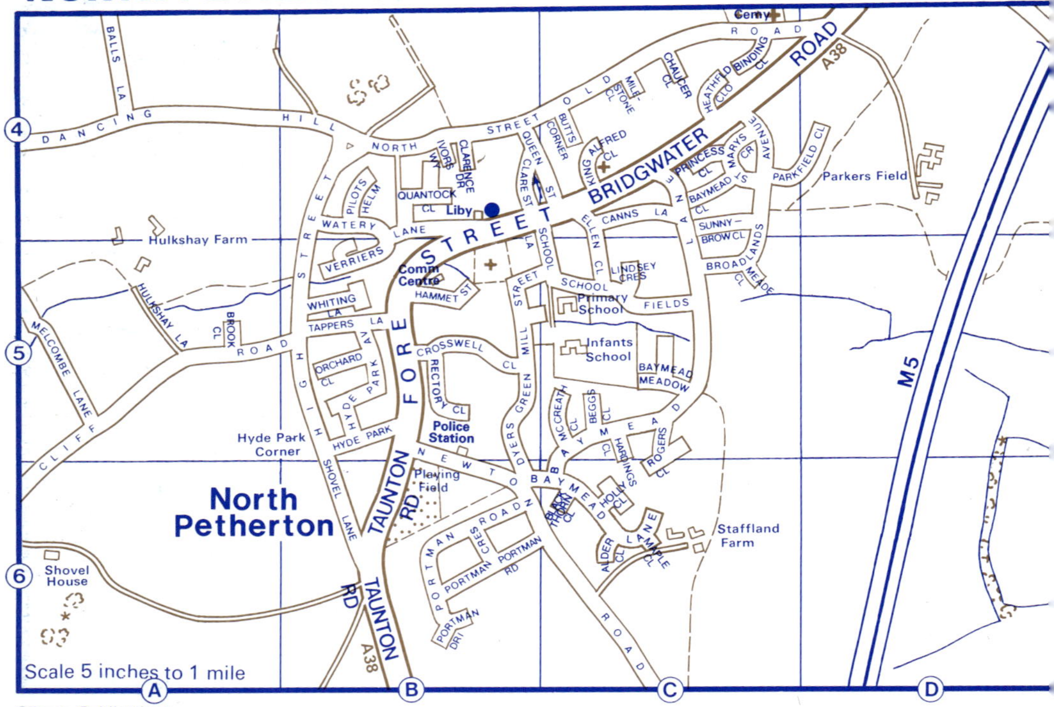

Hulkshay Farm
Parkers Field
Comm Centre
Primary School
Infants School
Police Station
Playing Field
Hyde Park Corner
North Petherton
Staffland Farm
Shovel House

Scale 5 inches to 1 mile

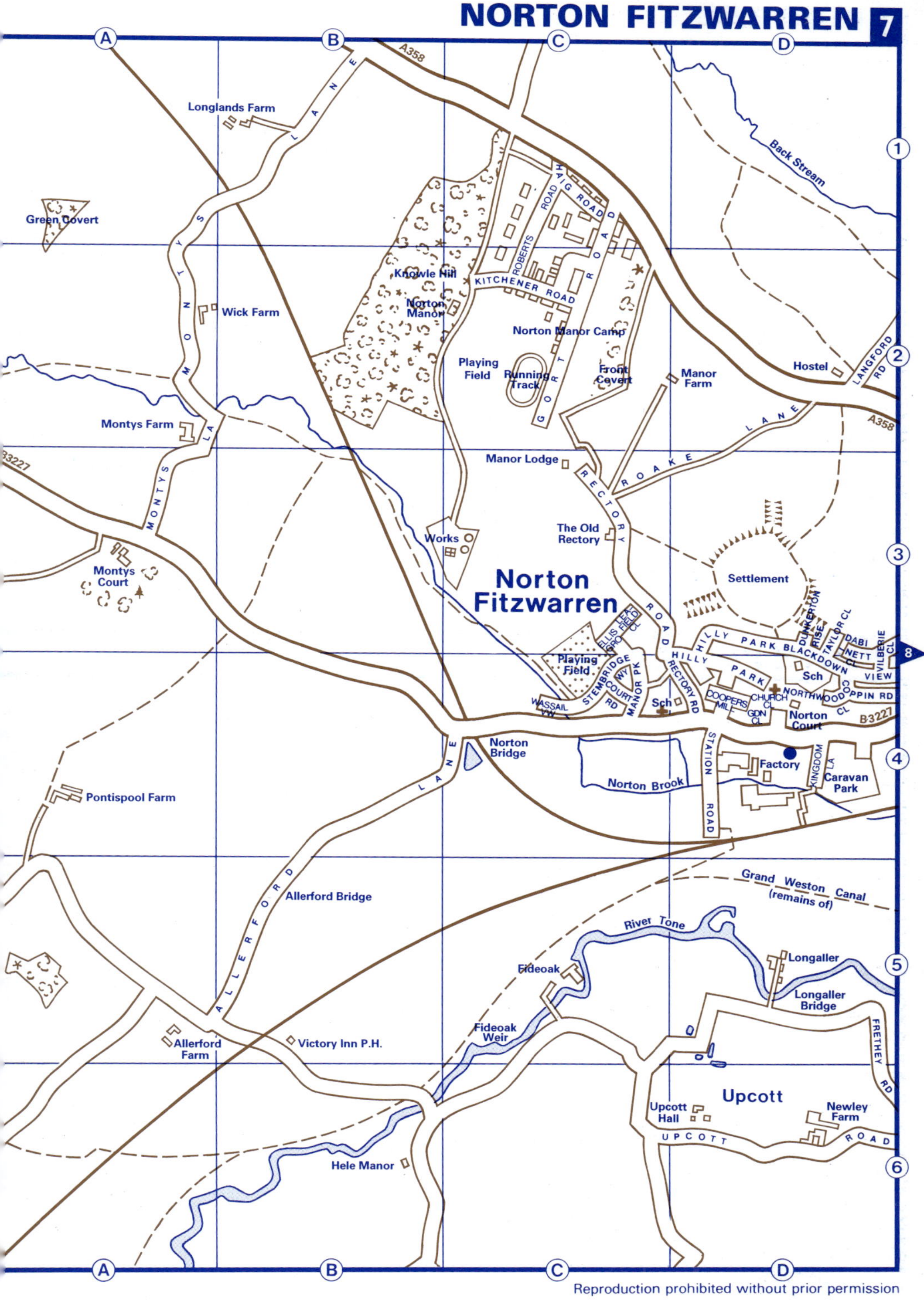
A
B
C
D
1
2
3
4
5
6
8
A358
Longlands Farm
LANE
Green Covert
MONTYS LA
Wick Farm
Knowle Hill
Norton Manor
HAIG ROAD
ROBERTS ROAD
KITCHENER ROAD
GORT ROAD
Norton Manor Camp
Playing Field
Running Track
Front Covert
Manor Farm
Back Stream
Hostel
LANGFORD RD
Montys Farm
B3227
MONTYS LA
Manor Lodge
ROAKE LANE
RECTORY ROAD
The Old Rectory
Works
Montys Court
Norton Fitzwarren
Settlement
ELLIS LEA
GROVE FIELD CL
HILLY PARK
BLACKDOWN
DUNKERTON RISE
TAYLOR CL
DABINETT CL
VILBERIE CL
VIEW
COPPIN RD
NORTHWOOD CL
Sch
Playing Field
STEMBRIDGE WY
COURT RD
MANOR PK
WASSAIL VW
Sch
RECTORY RD
COOPERS MILL
CHURCH CL
GDN CL
Norton Court
B3227
LANE
Norton Bridge
STATION ROAD
Factory
KINGDOM LA
Caravan Park
Norton Brook
Pontispool Farm
ALLERFORD
Allerford Bridge
Grand Weston Canal (remains of)
River Tone
Longaller
Longaller Bridge
Fideoak
Fideoak Weir
FRETHEY RD
Allerford Farm
Victory Inn P.H.
Upcott
Upcott Hall
Newley Farm
UPCOTT ROAD
Hele Manor

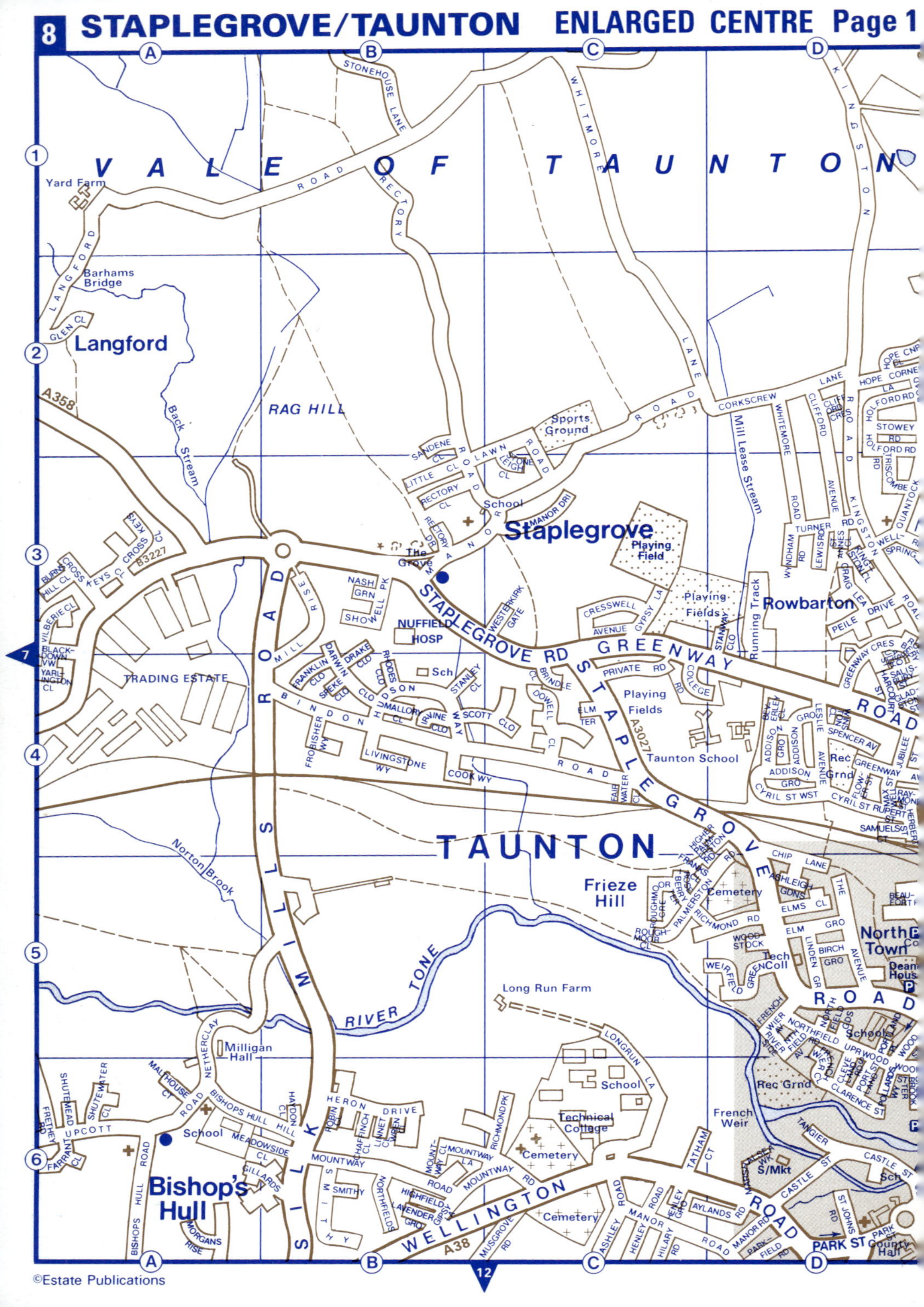

VALE OF TAUNTON
Yard Farm
LANGFORD
Barhams Bridge
GLEN CL
Langford
A358
RAG HILL
Back Stream
STONEHOUSE LANE
ROAD
RECTORY
WHITMORE
LANE
KINGSTON
CORKSCREW
Sports Ground
SANDENE CL
LITTLE CL
LAWN
STONELEIGH CL
RECTORY CL
School
MANOR DRI
Staplegrove
Playing Field
The Grove
KEYS CROSS
B3227
BURNS HILL CL
CROSS KEYS CL
VILBERIE CL
BLACKDOWN VW
YARLINGTON CL
TRADING ESTATE
NASH GRN
SHOWELL PK
NUFFIELD HOSP
STAPLEGROVE RD
WESTERKIRK GATE
GREENWAY
CRESSWELL AVENUE
GYPSY LA
Playing Fields
STANWAY CLO
Running Track
Mill Lease Stream
Rowbarton
WHITEMORE ROAD
CLIFFORD AVENUE
HOPE CNR CL
HOPE CORNER LA
HOLFORD RD
STOWEY RD
TRISCOMBE
QUANTOCK
TURNER RD
LEWIS RD
WYNDHAM RD
PEILE DRIVE
MILL RISE
FRANKLIN CLO
DARWIN CLO
DRAKE CLO
SPEKE CLO
RHODES CLO
HUDSON WAY
MALLORY CL
IRVINE CLO
SCOTT CLO
STANLEY CL
Sch
BINDON ROAD
FROBISHER WY
LIVINGSTONE WY
COOK WY
PRIVATE RD
BRINDLE CL
DOWELL CL
ELM TER
COLLEGE RD
FAIRWATER CL
A3027
Taunton School
ADDISON GRO
SPENCER AV
Rec Grnd
CYRIL ST WST
CYRIL ST
TAUNTON
Norton Brook
MILLS ROAD
Frieze Hill
Cemetery
RICHMOND RD
PALMERSTON
ROUGHMOOR CL
WOODSTOCK
Tech Coll
WEIRFIELD
GREENWAY
ASHLEIGH GDNS
ELMS CL
ELM GRO
LINDEN GR
BIRCH GRO
North Town
RIVER TONE
Long Run Farm
LONGRUN LA
Milligan Hall
NETHERCLAY
School
Technical College
Cemetery
FRENCH WEIR AV
NORTHFIELD RD
Rec Grnd
French Weir
SHUTEMEAD
SHUTEWATER CL
FRETHEY RD
UPCOTT
FARRANT CL
BISHOPS HULL HILL
MALTHOUSE CT
MEADOWSIDE CL
School
HAYDON CL
HERON DRIVE
ROBIN CL
CHAFFINCH CL
LINNET CL
WREN CL
RICHMOND PK
MOUNTWAY
MOUNTWAY CL
MOUNTWAY LA
Bishop's Hull
BISHOPS HULL ROAD
GILLARDS
MORGANS RISE
SILK MILLS
SMITHY
NORTHFIELDS
HIGHFIELD
LAVENDER GRO
WELLINGTON ROAD
A38
MUSGROVE RD
ASHLEY ROAD
MANOR ROAD
HENLEY
HILARY RD
AYLANDS RD
TATHAM CT
S/Mkt
TANGIER
CASTLE ST
PARK ST
County Hall
Sch

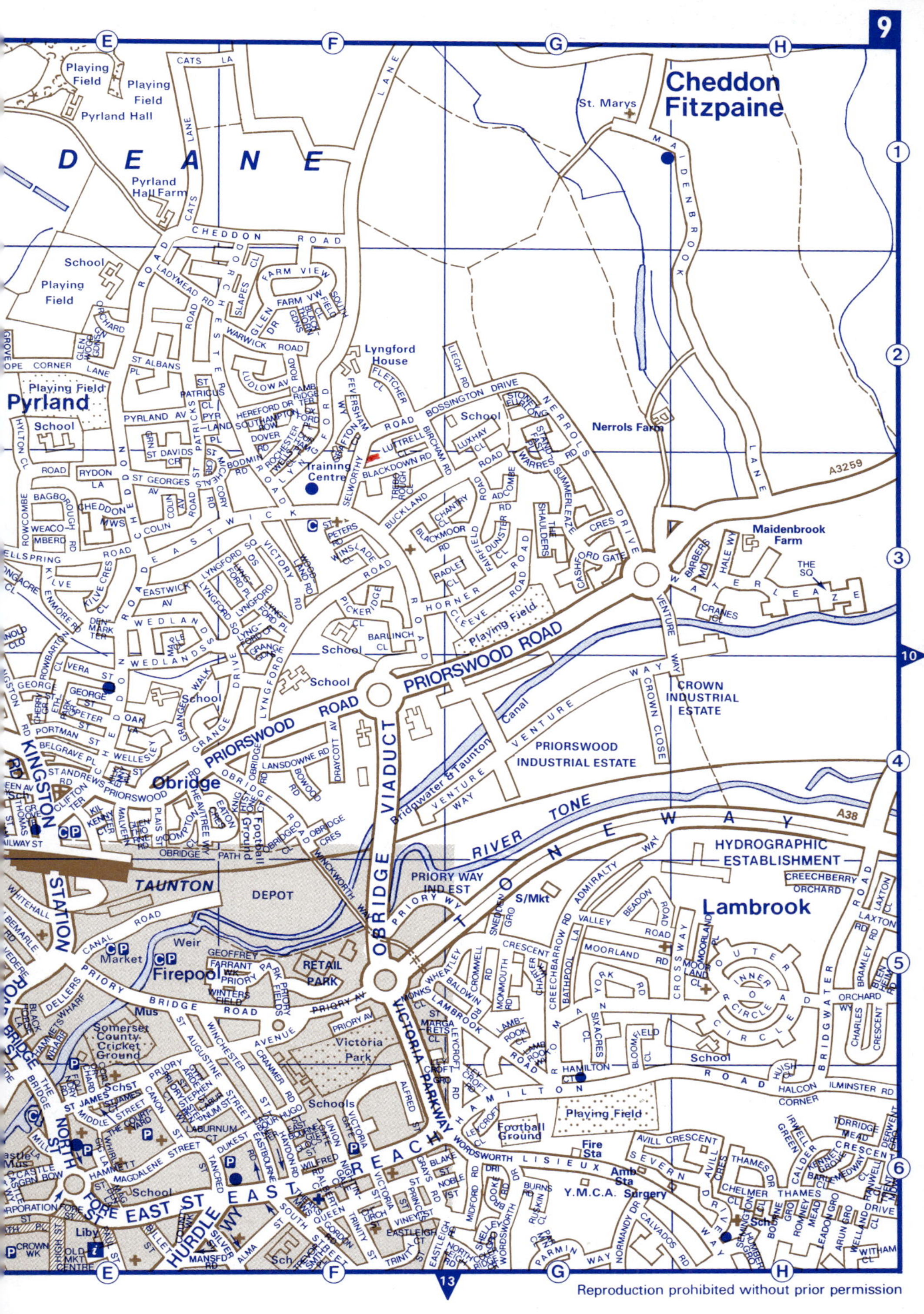

Cheddon Fitzpaine
St. Marys
DEANE
Pyrland Hall
Pyrland Hall Farm
Playing Field
School
Pyrland
Lyngford House
Training Centre
Nerrols Farm
Maidenbrook Farm
THE SQ
CHEDDON ROAD
MAIDENBROOK LANE
A3259
PRIORSWOOD ROAD
CROWN INDUSTRIAL ESTATE
PRIORSWOOD INDUSTRIAL ESTATE
Bridgwater & Taunton Canal
RIVER TONE
TONEWAY
A38
HYDROGRAPHIC ESTABLISHMENT
Obridge
OBRIDGE VIADUCT
TAUNTON
DEPOT
STATION
PRIORY WAY IND EST
S/Mkt
Lambrook
Firepool
Weir
Market
RETAIL PARK
PRIORY BRIDGE ROAD
Somerset County Cricket Ground
Victoria Park
VICTORIA PARKWAY
Schools
HAMILTON ROAD
Playing Field
Football Ground
Fire Sta
Amb Sta
Y.M.C.A.
Surgery
EAST REACH
EAST ST
HURDLE WY
Liby
LISIEUX WAY
10
13

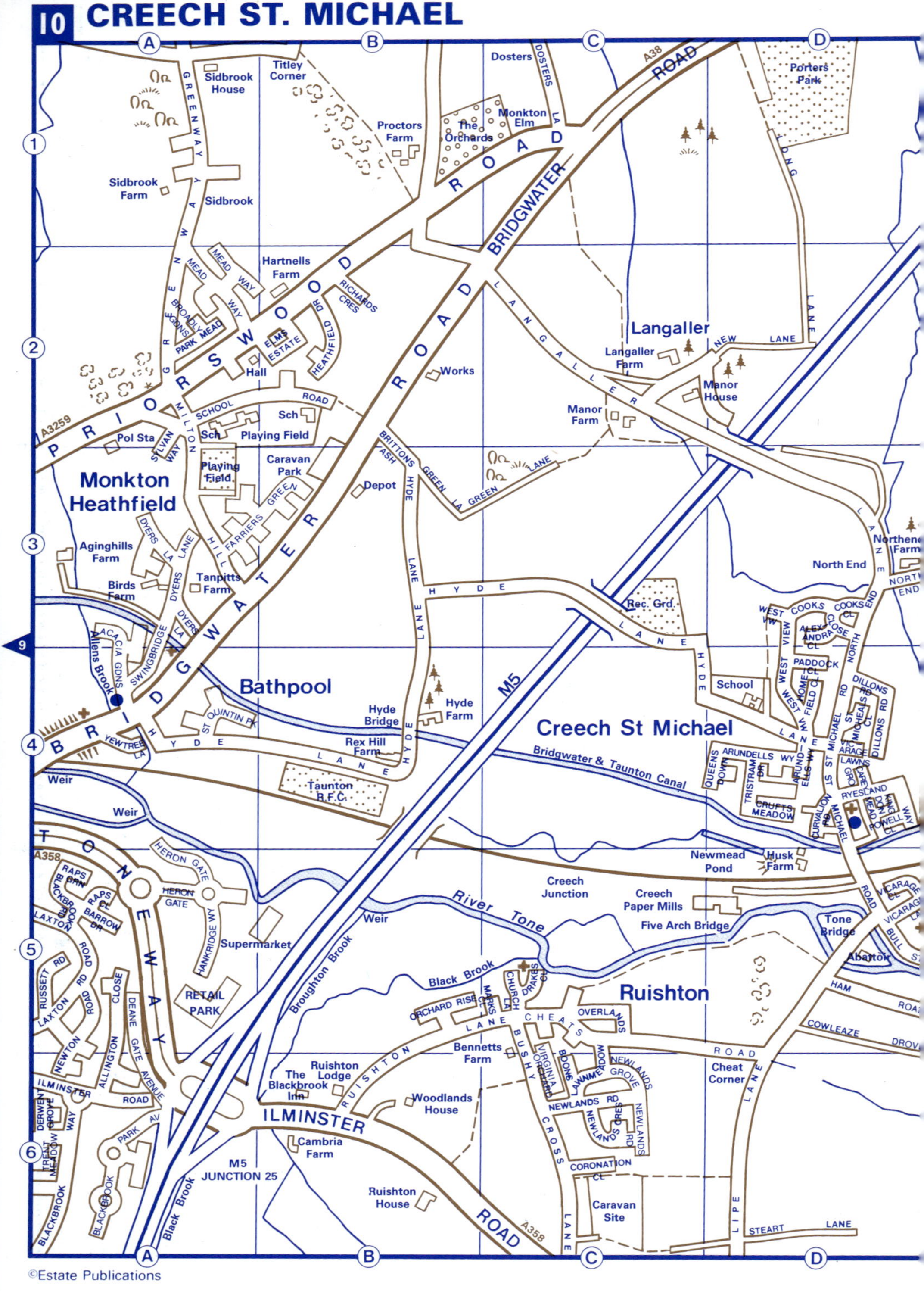
Monkton Heathfield
Creech St Michael
Bathpool
Ruishton
Langaller
Sidbrook House
Sidbrook Farm
Sidbrook
Titley Corner
Proctors Farm
Dosters
The Orchards
Monkton Elm
Porters Park
Hartnells Farm
PRIORSWOOD ROAD
BRIDGWATER ROAD
A38
A3259
Works
Langaller Farm
Manor House
Manor Farm
Pol Sta
Sch
Playing Field
Caravan Park
Depot
Aginghills Farm
Birds Farm
Tanpitts Farm
North End
Northend Farm
Rec. Grd.
School
Hyde Bridge
Hyde Farm
Rex Hill Farm
Taunton R.F.C.
Bridgwater & Taunton Canal
M5
Weir
Newmead Pond
Husk Farm
Creech Junction
Creech Paper Mills
Five Arch Bridge
Tone Bridge
Abattoir
River Tone
Supermarket
RETAIL PARK
Broughton Brook
Black Brook
Allens Brook
Bennetts Farm
Cheat Corner
The Blackbrook Inn
Ruishton Lodge
Woodlands House
ILMINSTER ROAD
A358
Cambria Farm
M5 JUNCTION 25
Ruishton House
Caravan Site
TONEWAY
CHEATS ROAD
STEART LANE
LIPE LANE
COWLEAZE DROVE
HAM ROAD
HYDE LANE
LANGALLER LANE
NEW LANE
LONG LANE
BRITTONS ASH
GREEN LA
MILTON HILL
SCHOOL ROAD
GREENWAY

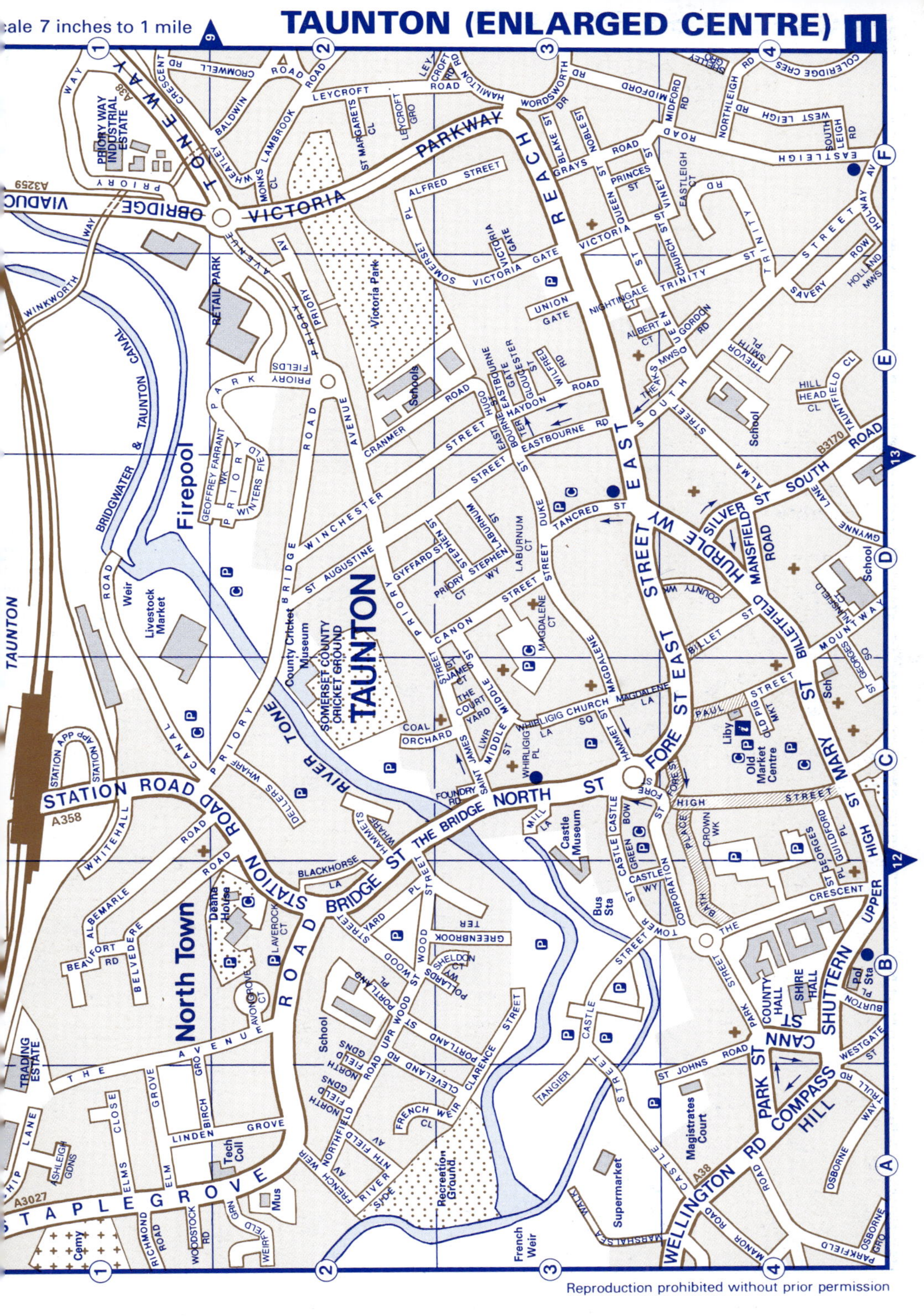

ENLARGED CENTRE Page 1

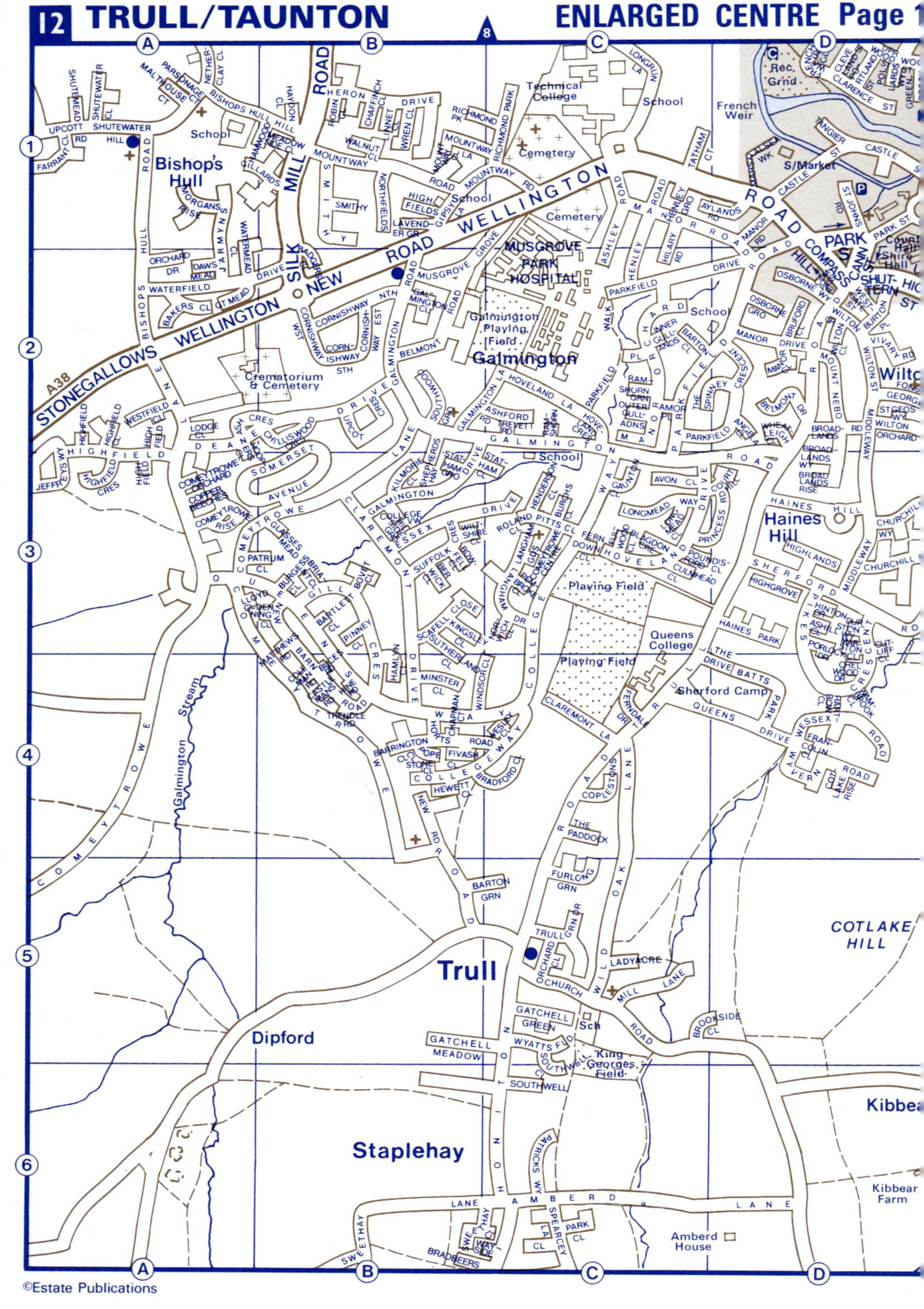

TAUNTON
Playing Field
Football Ground
Fire Station
Amb Sta
YMCA
Surgery
Victoria Park
Schools
Castle Museum
School
Liby
OLD PIG MKT CENTRE
Sch
Convent
Playing Field
VIVARY PARK
Golf Course
College
Playing Fields
STREAM-SIDE
Rec Ground
Sports Centre
Ash Meadows
Sherford
Sports Ground
Pool Farm
Cutliff Farm
Black Brook
Shoreditch Farm
Shoreditch
Timber Yard
Cornish Farm
Haygrass House
Orchard Portman House School
Longwater Bridge
St Michaels
Orchard Portman
TAUNTON RACECOURSE
M5
B3170
NORTH ST
FORE ST
EAST ST
EAST REACH
HIGH ST
MARY ST
SILVER ST
HURDLE WY
SOUTH ROAD
SOUTH ST
HAMILTON ROAD
WORDSWORTH DR
LISIEUX WAY
HOLWAY AV
HOLWAY RD
HOLWAY HILL
UPPER HOLWAY RD
CHESTNUT DR
SHOREDITCH ROAD
STOKE ROAD
BROUGHTON LANE
KILLAMS AVENUE
KILLAMS GREEN
BLACKBROOK WAY
WASHBOURNE WAY
AVILL CRESCENT
ILMINSTER RD
HALCON CORNER
CALWAY RD
MOUNT STREET
E
F
G
H
9
1
2
3
4
5
6

A - Z INDEX TO STREETS
with Postcodes

TAUNTON

Acacia Gdns. TA2 10 A3
Adcombe Rd. TA2 9 G3
Addison Gro. TA2 8 D4
Admiralty Way. TA1 9 G5
Albemarle Rd. TA1 11 B1
Albert Ct. TA1 11 E3
Alder Clo. TA1 13 H3
Alexandra Clo. TA3 10 D3
Alfred St. TA1 11 F2
Allerford La. TA4 7 B5
Allington Clo. TA1 10 A6
Alma St. TA1 11 D4
Alston Clo. TA1 12 C3
Amber Mead. TA1 13 H2
Amberd La. TA3 12 C6
Amor Pl. TA1 12 C2
Angela Clo. TA1 12 D2
Arnold Clo. TA2 9 E3
Arun Gro. TA1 9 H6
Arundells Way. TA3 10 D4
Ash Cres. TA1 12 A2
Ashbourne Cres. TA1 13 H2
Ashford Rd. TA1 12 C2
Ashill Clo. TA1 12 D3
Ashleigh Gdns. TA1 8 D5
Ashley Rd. TA1 12 C1
Asquith St. TA2 8 D4
Avill Cres. TA2 9 H6
Avon Clo. TA1 12 C3
Avongrove Ct. TA1 11 B2
Aylands Rd. TA1 12 D1
Bacon Dri. TA1 13 H2
Badgers Clo. TA1 12 B2
Bagborough Rd. TA2 9 E3
Bakers Clo. TA1 12 A2
Baldwin Rd. TA1 11 F2
Barbers Mead. TA2 9 H3
Barle Clo. TA1 9 H6
Barlinch Clo. TA2 9 F3
Barrington Clo. TA1 12 B4
Barrow Dri. TA1 10 A5
Bartlett Clo. TA1 12 B3
Barton Clo. TA1 12 C2
Barton Grn. TA3 12 B5
Bath Pl. TA1 11 B4
Bathpool La. TA1 9 G5
Batts Park. TA1 12 D4
Beadon Rd. TA1 9 G5
Beaufort Rd. TA1 11 B1
Belgrave Pl. TA2 9 E4
Belmont Dri. TA1 12 D2
Belmont Rd. TA1 12 B2
Belvedere Rd. TA1 11 B1
Berwick Clo. TA1 12 B3
Beverley Clo. TA2 8 D4
Bilberry Gro. TA1 13 G4
Billet St. TA1 11 D4
Billetfield. TA1 11 D4
Bindon Rd. TA2 8 B4
Birch Gro. TA1 11 A1
Bircham Rd. TA2 9 F2
Bishops Fox Dri. TA1 13 F3
Bishops Hull Hill. TA1 12 A1
Bishops Hull Rd. TA1 12 A2
Bishops Hull Rd. TA1 12 C1
Blackbrook Rd. TA1 10 A5
Blackbrook Way. TA1 13 H2
Blackdown Rd. TA2 9 F3
Blackdown View. TA2 7 D4
Blackhorse La. TA1 11 B2
Blackmoor Rd. TA2 9 G3
Blackthorn Gdns. TA2 9 F2
Blagdon Cres. TA1 12 C3
Blake St. TA1 11 F3
Blenheim Rd. TA1 9 H5
Bloomfield Clo. TA1 9 G5
Bluebell Clo. TA1 13 G4
Bodmin Rd. TA2 9 F3
Boons Orchard. TA3 10 C6
Bossington Dri. TA2 9 G2
Bourne Gro. TA1 9 H6
Bovet Clo. TA1 12 B3
Bowfell Clo. TA1 12 B3
Bowmont Gro. TA1 13 H2
Bowood Rd. TA2 9 F4
Bradbeers. TA3 12 B6
Bradford Clo. TA1 12 C4
Bramble Pk. TA1 13 G2
Bramley Rd. TA1 9 H5
Briant Clo. TA1 12 B3
Bridge St. TA1 11 B2
Bridgwater Rd. TA2 10 A4
Brindle Clo. TA2 8 C4
Brittons Ash. TA2 10 B3
Broadlands Rise. TA1 12 D3
Broadlands Rd. TA1 12 D2
Broadlands Way. TA1 12 D3
Broadly Gdns. TA2 10 A2
Broke Rd. TA1 13 G1
Brookside Clo. TA3 12 C5
Broughton Clo. TA1 13 G2
Broughton La. TA3 13 G5
Bruford Clo. TA1 12 D2
Buces Rd. TA1 12 B4
Buckland Rd. TA2 9 F3
Bull St. TA3 10 D5
Burchs Clo. TA1 12 C3
Burgess Clo. TA1 12 B3
Burns Rd. TA1 13 G1
Burnshill Clo. TA2 8 A3
Bushy Cross La. TA3 10 C6
Burton Pl. TA1 11 B4
Byron Rd. TA1 13 G2
Calder Cres. TA1 9 H6
Calvados Rd. TA1 13 G1
Calway Rd. TA1 13 F3
Cambridge Ter. TA2 9 F2
Campion Dri. TA1 13 G4
Canal Rd. TA1 11 C1
Cann St. TA1 11 B4
Canon St. TA1 11 D3
Cashford Gate. TA2 9 G3
Castle Bow. TA1 11 C3
Castle Grn. TA1 11 B3
Castle St. TA1 11 A4
Castle Way. TA1 11 B3
Castlemans Rd. TA1 12 B4
Cats La. TA2 9 E1
Cedar Clo. TA1 13 H2
Celandine Mead. TA1 13 G4
Chaffinch Clo. TA1 12 B1
Chantry Clo. TA2 9 G3
Chapman Ct. TA1 12 B4
Charles Cres. TA1 9 H5
Cheats Rd. TA3 10 C5
Charter Walk. TA1 9 G5
Cheddon Mews. TA2 9 E3
Cheddon Rd. TA2 9 E1
Chelmer Clo. TA1 9 H6
Chelwood Dri. TA1 12 D4
Cherry Gro. TA2 9 E4
Cherry Tree La. TA1 13 E3
Chestnut Dri. TA1 13 G3
Chilliswood Cres. TA1 12 B2
Chip La. TA1 11 A1
Church Clo. TA2 7 D4
Church La. TA3 10 C5
Church Rd. TA3 12 C5
Church Sq. TA1 11 C3
Church St. TA1 11 E4
Churchill Way. TA1 12 D3
Claremont Dri. TA1 12 B3
Claremont La. TA1 12 C4
Clarence St. TA1 11 A3
Cleeve Rd. TA2 9 G3
Cleveland Rd. TA1 11 A3
Clifford Av. TA2 8 D2
Clifford Cres. TA2 8 D2
Clifton Ter. TA2 9 E4
Clover Mead. TA1 13 G4
Coal Orchard. TA1 11 C3
Coleman Rd. TA1 12 B4
Coleridge Cres. TA1 11 F4
Colin Av. TA2 9 E3
Colin Rd. TA2 9 E3
College Rd. TA2 8 C4
College Vw. TA1 12 B3
College Way. TA1 12 B4
Comeytrowe Centre. TA1 12 C3
Comeytrowe La. TA1 12 A5
Comeytrowe Orch. TA1 12 A3
Comeytrowe Rise. TA1 12 A3
Comeytrowe Rd. TA1 12 A3
Compass Hill. TA1 11 A4
Compass Rise. TA1 12 D2
Compton Clo. TA2 9 E4
Cook Way. TA2 8 B4
Cooks Clo. TA3 10 D3
Cooks La. TA3 10 D3
Coopers Mill. TA2 7 D4
Coplestons. TA3 12 C4
Copper Beeches. TA1 12 A3
Coppin Rd. TA2 7 D4
Corkscrew La. TA2 8 D2
Cornishway East. TA1 12 B2
Cornishway Nth. TA1 12 B2
Cornishway Sth. TA1 12 B2
Cornishway West. TA1 12 B2
Coronation Clo. TA3 10 C6
Corporation St. TA1 11 B4
Cory Rd. TA2 9 F3
Cotlake Clo. TA1 13 E3
Cotlake Rise. TA1 12 D4
Country Walk. TA1 11 D4
Court Hill. TA1 12 D3
Court Rd. TA2 7 C4
Cowleaze Dro. TA3 10 D5
Craig Lea. TA2 8 D3
Cranes Clo. TA2 9 H3
Cranmer Rd. TA1 11 E2
Creechbarrow Rd. TA1 9 G5
Creechberry Orchard. TA1 9 H5
Crescent Way. TA1 13 E1
Cresswell Av. TA2 8 C3
Cromwell Rd. TA1 11 F2
Crosskeys Clo. TA2 8 A3
Crossway. TA1 9 H5
Crown Clo. TA2 9 G4
Crown Walk. TA1 9 E6
Crufts Meadow. TA3 10 D4
Culmhead Clo. TA1 12 C3
Curvalion Rd. TA3 10 D4
Cutliff Clo. TA1 12 D4
Cyril St. TA2 8 D4
Cyril St West. TA2 8 D4
Dabinett Clo. TA2 7 D3
Darwin Clo. TA2 8 B4
Daws Mead. TA1 12 A2
Deane Dri. TA1 12 A2
Dellers Wharf. TA1 11 C2
Denmark Ter. TA2 9 E3
Denning Clo. TA1 12 B3
Derwent Gro. TA1 10 A6
Dillons Rd. TA3 10 D4
Dorchester Rd. TA2 9 F2
Dosters La. TA2 10 C1
Dover Rd. TA2 9 F2
Dowell Clo. TA2 8 C4
Dowsland Way. TA1 13 G4
Drake Clo. TA2 8 B3
Drakes Clo. TA3 10 C5
Draycott Av. TA2 9 F4
Duke St. TA1 11 D3
Dunkerton Rise. TA2 7 D3
Dunkleys Way. TA1 13 G2
Dunster Clo. TA2 9 G3
Durham Pl. TA2 9 F2
Durston Way. TA1 12 D3
Dyers La. TA2 10 A3
East Reach. TA1 11 D3
East St. TA1 11 D4
Eastbourne Gate. TA1 11 E3
Eastbourne Rd. TA1 11 E3
Eastbourne Ter. TA1 11 E3
Eastleigh Ct. TA1 11 F4
Eastleigh Rd. TA1 11 F4
Eastwick Av. TA2 9 E3
Eastwick Rd. TA2 9 E3
Eaton Cres. TA2 9 F4
Ellis Gro. TA2 7 C3
Elm Gro. TA1 11 A1
Elm Ter. TA2 8 C4
Elms Clo. TA1 11 A1
Elms Est. TA2 10 B2
Enmore Rd. TA2 9 E3
Essex Dri. TA1 12 B3
Ethpark Gro. TA2 9 E4
Fairfield Rd. TA2 9 G3
Fairwater Clo. TA2 8 C4
Farm View. TA2 9 F2
Farrant Clo. TA1 12 A1
Farriers Grn. TA2 10 A3
Ferndale Dri. TA1 12 C4
Ferndown Clo. TA1 12 C3
Feversham Way. TA2 9 F2
Fivash Clo. TA1 12 B4
Fletcher Clo. TA2 9 F2
Flower St. TA2 8 D4
Fons George. TA1 12 D2
Fons George Rd. TA1 13 E3
Footlands Clo. TA1 13 E3
Fore St. TA1 11 C3
Foundry Rd. TA1 11 C3
Fouracres. TA1 13 F3
Francolin Clo. TA1 12 D4
Franklin Clo. TA2 8 B4
Franks Clo. TA1 8 C5
Fremantle Rd. TA1 13 F3
French Weir Av. TA1 11 A2
French Weir Clo. TA1 11 A2
Frethey Rd. TA4 7 D5
Frobisher Way. TA2 8 B4
Frys Mews. TA1 13 G3
Fullands Av. TA1 13 G4
Fullands Rd. TA1 13 G4
Fulwood Clo. TA1 12 C3
Furlong Grn. TA3 12 C5
Galmington Clo. TA1 12 B2
Galmington Dri. TA1 12 B3
Galmington La. TA1 12 B2
Galmington Rd. TA1 12 B2
Garden Clo. TA2 7 D4
Gatchell Grn. TA3 12 C5
Gatchell Meadow. TA3 12 B5
Gaunton Clo. TA1 12 C3
Geoffrey Farrant Wk. TA1 11 D1
George St. TA2 9 E4
Georges Mews. TA1 13 G3
Gill Cres. TA1 12 B3
Gillards. TA1 12 B1
Gipsy La. TA1 12 B1
Gladstone St. TA2 8 D4
Glasses Mead. TA1 12 B3
Glen Clo. TA2 8 A2
Glen Dri. TA2 9 F2
Glenthorne Rd. TA2 9 E4
Glenwood Gdns. TA2 9 E2
Gloucester St. TA1 11 E3
Gordon Rd. TA1 11 E4
Gordons Clo. TA1 13 F4
Gort Rd. TA2 7 C2
Grafton Clo. TA2 9 F2
Grange Dri. TA2 9 E4
Grange Gdns. TA2 9 F3
Grange Walk. TA2 9 E4
Grays Rd. TA1 11 F3
Great Mead. TA1 12 A2
Green La. TA2 10 B3
Greenbrook Ter. TA1 11 B3
Greenlands. TA1 13 F3
Greenway. TA2 10 A1
Greenway Av. TA2 8 D4
Greenway Cres. TA2 8 D4
Greenway Rd. TA2 8 C3
Grove Dri. TA2 9 E2
Grove Ter. TA2 9 E4
Guildford Pl. TA1 11 C4
Gwynne La. TA1 11 D4
Gyffard St. TA1 11 D2
Gypsy La. TA2 8 C3
Haig Rd. TA2 7 C1
Haines Hill. TA1 12 D3
Haines Park. TA1 12 D3
Halcon Cnr. TA1 9 H6
Hale Way. TA2 9 H3
Ham Rd. TA3 10 D5
Hamilton Ct. TA1 9 G5
Hamilton Rd. TA1 11 F3
Hamlyn Clo. TA1 12 B4
Hammet St. TA1 11 C3
Hammets Walk. TA1 13 E2
Hammets Wharf. TA1 11 C2
Hamwood. TA1 12 B1
Hankridge Way. TA1 10 A5
Harcourt St. TA2 8 D4
Harnell Clo. TA1 13 H2
Harp Chase. TA1 13 G3
Hartley Way. TA1 13 H2
Hartrow Clo. TA1 12 D4
Hawthorne Rd. TA1 13 H3
Haydon Clo. TA1 12 B1
Haydon Rd. TA1 11 E3
Haywood. TA1 13 H2
Hazel Clo. TA1 13 H3
Heather Clo. TA1 13 G4
Heathfield Dri. TA2 10 B2
Heavitree Way. TA2 9 E4
Henderson Clo. TA1 12 C3
Henley Gro. TA1 12 C1
Henley Rd. TA1 12 C2
Herbert St. TA2 8 D4
Hereford Dri. TA2 9 F2
Heron Dri. TA1 12 B1
Herons Gate. TA1 10 A5
Hewett Clo. TA1 12 B4
High St. TA1 11 C4
Higher Palmerston Rd. TA1 8 D5
Highfield. TA1 12 A2
Highfield Clo. TA1 12 A2
Highfield Cres. TA1 12 A3
Highfields. TA1 12 B1
Highgrove. TA1 12 D3
Highlands. TA1 12 D3
Hilary Rd. TA1 12 C1
Hill Head Clo. TA1 11 E4
Hillside Gro. TA1 12 B3
Hilly Park. TA2 7 D3
Hillyfields. TA1 13 G2
Hinton Dri. TA1 12 D3
Holford Rd. TA2 8 D2
Holland Mews. TA1 13 F2
Holly Clo. TA1 13 H3
Holway Av. TA1 11 F4
Holway Deane. TA1 13 H2
Holway Grn. TA1 13 H3
Holway Hill. TA1 13 G2
Holway Rd. TA1 13 F2
Homefield Clo. TA3 10 D4
Honiton Rd. TA3 12 C6
Hoopers Clo. TA1 12 A3
Hope Corner Clo. TA2 8 D2
Hope Corner La. TA2 8 D2
Hornbeam Rd. TA1 13 H3
Horner Rd. TA2 9 G3
Horts Rd. TA1 12 B4
Hoveland Cres. TA1 12 C2
Hoveland Dri. TA1 12 C3
Hoveland La. TA1 12 C2
Hudson Way. TA2 8 B4
Hugo St. TA1 11 E3
Huish Clo. TA1 9 H6
Humber Gro. TA1 13 H1
Hurdle Way. TA1 11 D4
Hyde La. TA2 10 A4
Hyde La. TA3 10 C4
Hylton Clo. TA2 9 E2
Ilminster Rd. TA3 10 B6
Ilminster Rd. TA1 9 H6
INDUSTRIAL & RETAIL:
Crown Ind Est. TA2 9 G4
Priorswood Ind Est. TA2 9 G4
Priory Way Ind Est. TA1 11 F1
Inner Circle. TA1 9 H5
Inner Gullands. TA1 12 C2
Irvine Clo. TA2 8 B4
Irwell Grn. TA1 9 H6
James Walk. TA1 13 G2
Jarmyns. TA1 12 A2
Jeffreys Way. TA1 12 A3
Jubilee St. TA2 8 D4
Juniper Rd. TA1 13 G3
Keats Rd. TA1 13 G2
Kennet Gro. TA1 9 H6
Kenwyn Clo. TA1 13 H2
Kilkenny Av. TA2 9 E4
Kilkenny Ct. TA2 9 E4
Killams Av. TA1 13 F4
Killams Clo. TA1 13 G4
Killams Cres. TA1 13 F4
Killams Grn. TA1 13 F5
Killams La. TA1 13 F4
Kilmorie Clo. TA1 12 B3
Kilve Clo. TA2 9 E3
Kilve Cres. TA2 9 E3
Kingdom La. TA2 7 D4
Kings Clo. TA1 13 F2
Kingsley Clo. TA1 12 B3
Kingston Clo. TA2 8 D3
Kingston Rd. TA2 8 D1
Kingsway. TA1 13 F4
Kitchener Rd. TA2 7 C2
Knightstone Ct. TA2 9 F4
Laburnum Ct. TA1 11 D3
Laburnum St. TA1 11 D3
Ladyacre. TA3 12 C5
Ladymead Rd. TA2 9 E2
Lambrook Clo. TA1 9 G5
Lambrook Rd. TA1 11 F2
Lambrook Way. TA1 9 G5
Langaller La. TA2 10 C2
Langford Rd. TA2 8 A2
Langham Dri. TA1 12 C3
Langham Gdns. TA1 12 C3
Lansdowne Rd. TA2 9 F4
Larch Clo. TA1 13 H3
Larkspur Clo. TA1 13 G4
Laurel Clo. TA1 13 G3
Lavender Gro. TA1 12 B1
Laverock Ct. TA1 11 B2
Lawn Rd. TA2 8 C2
Lawnmeadow. TA3 10 C6
Laxton Clo. TA1 9 H5
Laxton Rd. TA1 9 H5
Leadon Gro. TA1 9 H6
Leafield Clo. TA2 7 C3
Leigh Rd. TA2 9 G2
Leslie Av. TA2 8 D4
Lewis Rd. TA2 8 D3
Leycroft Clo. TA1 9 G6
Leycroft Gro. TA1 11 F2
Leycroft Rd. TA1 11 F2
Lilac Clo. TA1 13 H3
Lime Cres. TA1 13 G3
Linden Gro. TA1 11 A1
Linnet Clo. TA1 12 B1
Lipe La. TA3 10 D6
Lisieux Way. TA1 13 G1
Little Clo. TA2 8 B3
Livingstone Way. TA2 8 B4
Lloyd Clo. TA1 12 A3
Lodge Clo. TA1 12 A2
Long La. TA2 10 D1
Longacre Clo. TA2 9 E3
Longmead Clo. TA1 12 C3
Longmead Way. TA1 12 C3
Longrun La. TA1 8 C5
Lower Holway Clo. TA1 13 H2
Ludlow Av. TA2 9 F2
Luttrell Clo. TA2 9 F2
Luxhay Clo. TA2 9 G2
Lyngford Cres. TA2 9 F3

—Kirke Grove 9F3

Lyngford La. TA2 9 F3
Lyngford Pl. TA2 9 F3
Lyngford Rd. TA2 9 F4
Lyngford Sq. TA2 9 F3
Lynor Clo. TA1 13 H2
Magdalene Ct. TA1 11 C3
Magdalene La. TA1 11 C3
Magdelene St. TA1 11 C3
Maidenbrook La. TA2 9 H1
Mallory Clo. TA2 8 B4
Malthouse Ct. TA1 12 A1
Malvern Ter. TA2 9 E4
Manor Clo. TA1 12 D2
Manor Dri. TA2 8 C3
Manor Dri. TA1 12 D2
Manor Orchard. TA1 12 C2
Manor Orchard Pl. TA1 12 C2
Manor Park. TA2 7 C4
Manor Rd. TA1 11 A4
Manor Rd. TA2 8 B3
Mansfield Rd. TA1 11 D4
Maple Clo. TA2 9 E3
Marden Gro. TA1 13 H2
Marks Clo. TA3 10 C5
Marshalsea Wk. TA1 11 A3
Marston Clo. TA1 12 D4
Martins. TA3 10 C5
Mary St. TA1 11 C4
Matthews Rd. TA1 12 B4
Maxwell St. TA2 8 D4
Mead Way. TA2 10 A2
Meadowside Clo. TA1 12 B1
Medway Clo. TA1 9 H6
Middle St. TA1 11 C3
Middleway. TA1 12 D2
Midford Rd. TA1 11 F3
Mill La. TA1 11 C3
Mill La, Trull. TA3 12 C5
Mill Rise. TA2 8 B3
Milton Clo. TA1 13 G2
Milton Hill. TA2 10 A3
Milton Rd. TA1 13 G2
Minster Clo. TA1 12 B4
Monks Clo. TA1 11 F2
Monmouth Rd. TA1 9 G5
Montys La. TA4 7 A3
Moorland Clo. TA1 9 G5
Moorland Pl. TA1 9 H5
Moorland Rd. TA1 9 G5
Morgans Rise. TA1 12 A1
Mount Nebo Rd. TA1 12 D2
Mount St. TA1 13 E2
Mountfields Av. TA1 13 F3
Mountfields Pk. TA1 13 F3
Mountfields Rd. TA1 13 F3
Mountway. TA1 11 D4
Mountway Clo. TA1 12 B1
Mountway La. TA1 12 B1
Mountway Rd. TA1 12 B1
Mulberry Clo. TA1 13 G3
Musgrove Clo. TA1 12 B2
Nash Grn. TA2 8 B3
Nerrols Dri. TA1 9 G2
Netherclay Clo. TA1 12 A1
New Barn Rd. TA1 12 B3
New La. TA1 10 D2
New Rd. TA3 12 B4
Newlands Cres. TA3 10 C6
Newlands Rd. TA3 10 C6
Newton Rd. TA1 10 A5
Nightingale Ct. TA1 11 E3
Noble St. TA1 11 F3
Normandy Dri. TA1 13 G2
North End. TA3 10 D4
North St. TA1 11 C3
Northfield Av. TA1 11 A2
Northfield Gdns. TA1 11 A2
Northfield Rd. TA1 11 A2
Northfields. TA1 12 B1
Northwood Clo. TA2 7 D4
Norwich Clo. TA1 12 C3
Nunsfield Ct. TA1 11 D4
Oak La. TA2 9 E4
Obridge Clo. TA2 9 F4
Obridge Cres. TA2 9 F4
Obridge Path. TA2 9 E4
Obridge Rd. TA2 9 F4
Obridge Viaduct. TA2 11 F1
Old Market Centre. TA1 9 E6
Old Pig Mkt. TA1 11 C4
Orchard Clo, Holway. TA1 13 G4
Orchard Clo, Trull. TA3 12 C5
Orchard Dri. TA1 12 A2
Orchard Grn. TA2 9 E2
Orchard Rise. TA3 10 B5
Orchard Way. TA1 9 H5
Osborne Gro. TA1 11 A4
Osborne Way. TA1 11 A4
Outer Circle. TA1 9 H5
Outer Gullands. TA1 12 C2
Overlands. TA3 10 C5
Oxford Pl. TA2 9 F2
Paddock Clo. TA3 10 D4
Palmerston Rd. TA1 8 C5
Park Clo. TA3 12 C6
Park Mead. TA2 10 A2
Park St. TA1 11 A4
Parkfield Cres. TA1 12 C2
Parkfield Dri. TA1 12 C2
Parkfield Rd. TA1 11 A4
Parkfield Walk. TA1 12 C2
Parmin Clo. TA1 13 G1
Parmin Way. TA1 13 G2
Parrett Mead. TA1 13 H2
Parsonage Ct. TA1 12 A1
Patricks Way. TA3 12 C6
Patrum Clo. TA1 12 B3
Paul St. TA1 11 C4
Peile Dri. TA2 8 D3
Pembroke Clo. TA1 12 C3
Peter St. TA2 9 E4
Pickeridge Clo. TA2 9 F3
Pikes Cres. TA1 12 D3
Pine Clo. TA1 13 H3
Pinney Clo. TA1 12 B3
Pitts Clo. TA1 12 C3
Plais St. TA2 9 E4
Pollards Way. TA1 11 B3
Pope Clo. TA1 12 B4
Poplar Rd. TA1 13 H3
Porlock Dri. TA1 12 D3
Portland Pl. TA1 11 B2
Portland St. TA1 11 B3
Portman St. TA2 9 E4
Poundisford Clo. TA1 12 C3
Princes St. TA1 11 F3
Princess Rd. TA1 12 C3
Priorswood Rd. TA2 9 E4
Priory Av. TA1 11 D2
Priory Bridge Rd. TA1 11 C2
Priory Ct. TA1 11 D3
Priory Fields. TA1 11 E2
Priory Pk. TA1 11 D2
Private Rd. TA2 8 C4
*Prowses Mdw, Kingdom La. TA2 7 D4
Pyrland Av. TA2 9 E2
Pyrland Pl. TA2 9 E2
Quantock Rd. TA2 8 D3
Queen St. TA1 11 E4
Queens Down. TA3 10 D4
Queens Dri. TA1 12 D4
Queens Way. TA1 12 A3
Radlet Clo. TA2 9 G3
Railway St. TA2 11 B1
Ramshorn. TA1 12 C2
Ramshorn Grn. TA1 12 C2
Ranwell Clo. TA1 9 H6
Raps Clo. TA1 10 A5
Raps Grn. TA1 10 A5
Raymond St. TA2 8 D4
Rectory Clo. TA2 8 B3
Rectory Dri. TA2 8 B3
Rectory Rd, Norton Fitzwarren. TA2 7 C3
Rectory Rd, Staplegrove. TA2 8 B1
Redlake Dri. TA1 13 H2
Rhodes Clo. TA2 8 B4
Richards Cres. TA2 10 B2
Richmond Pk. TA1 12 C1
Richmond Rd. TA1 11 A1
River Side. TA1 11 A2
Roake La. TA2 7 C3
Roberts Rd. TA2 7 C2
Robin Clo. TA1 12 B1
Rochester Rd. TA2 9 F2
Roland Clo. TA1 12 C3
Roman Rd. TA1 9 G5
Romney Mead. TA1 9 H6
Roseberry Ter. TA1 8 C5
Rosebery St. TA2 8 D3
Roughmoor Clo. TA1 8 C5
Roughmoor Cres. TA1 8 C5
Rowan Dri. TA1 13 H3
Rowbarton Clo. TA2 9 E4
Rowcombe Rd. TA2 9 E3
Ruishton La. TA3 10 B6
Rupert St. TA2 8 D4
Ruskin Clo. TA1 13 G1
Russett Rd. TA1 10 A5
Ryburn Clo. TA1 13 H2
Rydon La. TA1 9 E3
Saffron Clo. TA1 13 G4
St Albans Pl. TA2 9 E2
St Andrews Rd. TA2 9 E4
St Annes Clo. TA2 8 D3
St Augustine St. TA1 11 D2
St Davids Clo. TA2 9 E3
St Davids Grn. TA2 9 E2
St Georges Av. TA2 9 E3
St Georges Pl. TA1 11 B4
St Georges Sq. TA1 11 C4
St Georges Way. TA1 12 D2
St James Ct. TA1 11 C3
St James St. TA1 11 C3
St Johns Rd. TA1 11 B4
St Margarets Clo. TA1 11 F2
St Michael Rd. TA3 10 D4
St Michaels Clo. TA3 10 D4
St Michaels Cres. TA2 9 E3
St Patricks Rd. TA2 9 E3
St Patricus Clo. TA2 9 E2
St Peters Rd. TA2 9 F3
St Quentin Pk. TA2 10 A4
Salisbury St. TA2 8 D4
Samuels Ct. TA2 8 D4
Sandene Clo. TA2 8 B2
Savery Row. TA1 11 E4
Scafell Clo. TA1 12 B3
School Rd. TA2 10 A2
Scott Clo. TA2 8 C3
Selworthy Rd. TA2 9 F3
Semington Clo. TA1 13 H1
Severn Dri. TA1 13 H1
Shakespeare Av. TA1 13 G2
Sheldon Ct. TA1 11 B3
Shelley Gro. TA1 11 F4
Shepherds Hay. TA1 12 B3
Sherford Rd. TA1 12 D3
Shoreditch Rd. TA1 13 G3
Showell Park. TA2 8 B3
Shutemead. TA1 12 A1
Shutewater Clo. TA1 12 A1
Shutewater Hill. TA1 12 A1
Shuttern. TA1 11 B4
Silk Mill Rd. TA1 12 B2
Silver St. TA1 11 D4
Sixacres Ct. TA1 9 G5
Slapes Clo. TA2 9 F2
Smithy. TA1 12 B1
Sneddon Gro. TA1 9 G5
Somerset Av. TA1 12 B3
Somerset Pl. TA1 11 E3
South Rd. TA1 11 D4
South St. TA1 11 E3
Southampton Row. TA2 9 F2
Southfield Clo. TA2 9 F2
Southwell. TA3 12 C6
Southleigh Rd. TA1 11 F4
Southwell Clo. TA3 12 C6
Southwood Gro. TA1 12 B2
Spearcey Clo. TA3 12 C6
Spearcey La. TA3 12 C6
Speke Clo. TA2 8 B4
Spencer Av. TA2 8 D4
Standfast Pl. TA2 9 G2
Stanley Clo. TA2 8 B4
Stanway Clo. TA2 8 D3
Staplegrove Rd. TA1 11 A1
Statham Clo. TA1 12 C3
Statham Gro. TA1 12 B3
Station App. TA1 11 C1
Station Rd. TA1 11 B2
Station Rd. TA2 7 D4
Steart La. TA3 10 D6
Stembridge Way. TA2 7 C4
Stephen St. TA1 11 D3
Stephen Way. TA1 11 D3
Stoke La. TA3 13 H4
Stoke Rd. TA1 13 G3
Stone Clo. TA1 12 B4
Stonegallows. TA1 12 A2
Stonehouse La. TA2 8 B1
Stoneleigh Clo. TA2 8 C3
Stoney Furlong. TA2 9 G2
Stowey Rd. TA2 8 D2
Streamside. TA1 13 G2
Suffolk Cres. TA1 12 B3
Summerleaze Cres. TA2 9 G3
Sundew Clo. TA1 13 G4
Sutherland Clo. TA1 12 B3
Sweethay Clo. TA3 12 C6
Sweethay La. TA3 12 B6
Swingbridge. TA2 10 A4
Sycamore Clo. TA1 13 G3
Sylvan Way. TA2 10 A2
Tamar Av. TA1 13 G4
Tancred St. TA1 11 D3
Tangier. TA1 11 B3
Tatham Ct. TA1 8 C6
Tauntfield Clo. TA1 11 E4
Taylor Clo. TA2 7 D3
Thames Dri. TA1 9 H6
The Avenue. TA1 11 A1
The Bridge. TA1 11 C3
The Courtyard. TA1 11 C3
The Crescent. TA1 11 B4
The Drive. TA1 12 D4
The Fairways. TA1 13 E3
The Oaks. TA1 13 G3
The Paddock, Holway. TA1 13 G4
The Paddock, Trull. TA3 12 C4
The Shaulders TA2 9 G3
The Spinney. TA1 12 D2
The Square, Monkton Heathfield. TA2 9 H3
The Square, Taunton. TA1 13 G3
Theaks Mews. TA1 11 E3
Thomas St. TA2 9 E4
Toneway. TA1 11 F1
Torridge Mead. TA1 9 H6
Tower St. TA1 11 B3
Treborough Clo. TA2 9 F3
Trendle Rd. TA1 12 B4
Trent Meadow. TA1 10 A6
Trevett Rd. TA1 12 C2
Trevor Smith Pl. TA1 11 E4
Trinity Rd. TA1 11 E4
Trinity St. TA1 11 E4
Triscombe Rd. TA2 8 D3
Tristram Dri. TA3 10 D4
Trull Green Dri. TA3 12 C5
Trull Rd. TA1 11 A4
Turner Rd. TA2 8 D3
Tyne Park. TA1 13 H2
Union Gate. TA1 11 E3
Upcot Cres. TA1 12 B2
Upcot Rd. TA1 12 A1
Upper High St. TA1 11 B4
Upper Holway Rd. TA1 13 G2
Upper Wood St. TA1 11 B2
Valley Rd. TA1 9 G5
Venture Way. TA2 9 G4
Vera St. TA2 9 E4
Vicarage Clo. TA3 10 D5
Vicarage La. TA3 10 D5
Victoria Gate. TA1 11 E3
Victoria Parkway. TA1 11 F2
Victoria St. TA1 11 F3
Victory Rd. TA2 9 F3
Vilberie Clo. TA2 8 A3
Viney St. TA1 11 F3
Vivary Rd. TA1 12 D2
Walnut Clo. TA1 12 B1
Wambrook Clo. TA1 12 D4
Wansbeck Grn. TA1 13 H2
Warres Rd. TA2 9 G3
Warwick Gdns. TA1 13 H3
Warwick Rd. TA2 9 F2
Wassail View. TA2 7 C4
Waterfield Dri. TA1 12 A2
Waterleaze. TA2 9 H3
Watermead Clo. TA1 12 A2
Waveney Clo. TA1 13 H2
Wayside. TA3 12 C6
Weacombe Rd. TA1 9 E3
Wedlands. TA2 9 E3
Weirfield Grn. TA1 11 A1
Welland Clo. TA1 9 H6
Wellesley St. TA2 9 E4
Wellington New Rd. TA1 12 A2
Wellington Rd. TA1 11 A4
Wells Clo. TA2 9 F3
Wellspring Rd. TA2 8 D3
Wesley Clo. TA1 12 C4
Wessex Rd. TA1 12 D4
West View. TA3 10 D3
Westerkirk Gate. TA2 8 C3
Westfield Clo. TA1 12 A2
Westgate St. TA1 11 B4
Westleigh Rd. TA1 11 F4
Wheatleigh Clo. TA1 12 D2
Wheatley Cres. TA1 11 F1
Whirligig La. TA1 11 C3
Whirligig Pl. TA1 11 C3
Whitehall. TA1 11 C1
Whitemore Rd. TA2 8 D2
Whitmoor La. TA2 8 C1
Wild Oak La. TA3 12 C5
Wilfred Rd. TA1 11 E3
William St. TA2 9 E4
Willow Clo. TA1 13 H3
Wilton Clo. TA1 12 D2
Wilton Gro. TA1 12 D2
Wilton Lands. TA1 13 E2
Wilton Orchard. TA1 12 D2
Wilton St. TA1 12 D2
Wiltshire Clo. TA1 12 B3
Wimbourne Clo. TA1 13 H2
Winchester St. TA1 11 D2
Windsor Clo. TA1 12 B4
Winkworth Way. TA2 11 E1
Winslade Clo. TA2 9 F3
Winston Clo. TA2 8 D4
Winters Field. TA1 11 D2
Witham Clo. TA1 13 H1
Wood St. TA1 11 B2
Woodland Rd. TA2 9 F3
Woodrush Clo. TA1 13 G4
Woodstock Rd. TA1 11 A1
Wordsworth Dri. TA1 11 F3
Wren Clo. TA1 12 B1
Wyatts Field. TA3 12 C5
Wyndham Rd. TA2 8 D3
Wyvern Rd. TA1 12 D4
Yarde Pl. TA1 11 B2
Yarlington Clo. TA2 8 A4
Yewtree La. TA2 10 A4
York Rd. TA1 9 G5

BRIDGWATER/ SYDENHAM & WEMBDON

Adscombe Av. TA6 5 E2
Albert St. TA6 4 A4
Albion Clo. TA6 4 D2
Alderney Rd. TA6 5 E5
Alexandra Rd. TA6 4 A3
Alfoxton Rd. TA6 3 C4
All Saints Ter. TA6 4 D4
Allen Rd. TA6 4 B6
Almond Tree Clo. TA6 5 F4
Andersfield Clo. TA6 3 B4
Angel Cres. TA6 4 B3
Ansons Way. TA6 4 B2
Appletree Clo. TA6 5 F4
Apricot Tree Clo. TA6 5 F3
Arlington Clo. TA6 4 C6
Ash Clo. TA6 5 F3
Ashford Clo. TA6 4 A6
Ashgrove Way. TA6 5 F1
Ashleigh Av. TA6 4 C5
Ashleigh Ter. TA6 4 C5
Ashman Way. TA6 3 D4
Ashton Rd. TA6 4 B6
Athlone Rd. TA6 4 C6
Avalon Rd. TA6 5 E3
Avebury Dri. TA6 5 F3
Axe Rd. TA6 4 D5
Bagborough Dri. TA6 4 B6
Bailey St. TA6 4 D2
Barclay St. TA6 4 C3
Barham Clo. TA6 4 C1
Barrows Clo. TA6 4 A6
Bath Rd. TA6 4 D2
Bayford Rd. TA6 5 E1
Beckworth Clo. TA6 5 E5
Bedford Clo. TA6 5 E5
Beech Dri. TA6 5 F3
Beech Rd. TA6 5 F3
Beechwood. TA6 4 B6
Bell Clo. TA6 4 B2
Belmont Clo. TA6 3 B4
Berry Clo. TA6 4 A6
Berrydale Av. TA6 4 B2
Biddiscombe Clo. TA6 4 B6
Bincombe Rd. TA6 5 E4
Binford Pl. TA6 4 C3
Birch Clo. TA6 5 F3
Bircham Clo. TA6 3 C4
Blackdown Rd. TA6 5 E4
Blacklands. TA6 4 B3
Blake Pl. TA6 4 C3
Blake St. TA6 4 C3
Blakes La. TA5 3 C1
Blakes Rd. TA6 3 D1
Blenheim Clo. TA6 5 E1
Bloom Row. TA6 5 F2
Blossom Clo. TA6 5 E3
Boards Rd. TA6 4 C2
Bond St. TA6 4 B3
Boothway. TA6 4 A2
Bouverie Rd. TA6 3 D3
Bower Av. TA6 5 E1
Bower La. TA5 3 A4
Bower La. TA6 5 F1
Bowerings Rd. TA6 4 A6
Bradfield Clo. TA6 4 B6
Branksome Av. TA6 4 D2
Brantwood Rd. TA6 3 C2
Brendon Rd. TA6 4 B2
Brendon Way. TA6 4 B2
Bristol Rd. TA6 4 D2
Broadlands La. TA5 3 B4
Broadoak Rd. TA6 5 F2
Broadway. TA6 4 B4
Brooklands. TA6 5 E3
Brue Av. TA6 4 C5
Bryer Clo. TA6 4 B6
Brymore Clo. TA6 3 D3
Buckingham Clo. TA6 4 C6
Butleigh Clo. TA6 5 E3
Camden Rd. TA6 4 A3
Canal View. TA6 4 C4
Cannon Clo. TA6 4 D3
Capes Clo. TA6 4 C3
Caradon Pl. TA6 4 B1
Carlton Dri. TA6 4 B1
Carvers Rd. TA6 4 C3
Castle Moat. TA6 4 B3
Castle St. TA6 4 B3
Cedar Clo. TA6 5 E4
Chamberlin Av. TA6 5 E2
Chandos St. TA6 4 B3
Chapel St. TA6 4 C3
Charlton Clo. TA6 5 E3
Charnwood Clo. TA6 4 B1
Chatham Av. TA6 4 B2
Chedzoy La. TA7 5 G1
Chepstow Av. TA6 4 C6
Cherry Clo. TA6 5 E4
Chestnut Clo. TA6 5 E4
Chidgey Clo. TA6 4 B2
Chilton Clo. TA6 4 B1
Chilton St. TA6 4 B1
Church Path. TA6 4 A2
Church Rd. TA6 3 D2
Church St. TA6 4 C3
Clare St. TA6 4 B3
Claremont Gro. TA6 5 F2
Clarks Rd. TA6 4 D4
Cloverton Rd. TA6 5 F1
Coleridge Grn. TA6 4 A2
Coleridge Rd. TA6 4 A2
Coleridge Sq. TA6 4 A2
College Way. TA6 4 D2

Colley La. TA6 4 D4
Collingwood Ct. TA6 4 B2
Colmer Rd. TA6 4 B1
Condell Clo. TA6 4 B1
Cormorant Clo. TA6 5 E4
Cornborough Pl. TA6 4 D3
Cornhill. TA6 4 B3
Coronation Rd. TA6 4 A3
Cothelstone Clo. TA6 3 B4
Court St. TA6 4 B3
Courtway Av. TA6 5 E4
Cranbourne Clo. TA6 4 B1
Cranleigh Gdns. TA6 4 C3
Cranworth Way. TA6 5 E5
Crestfield Av. TA6 4 B1
Cromwell Rd. TA6 4 C5
Crossacre. TA6 3 D2
Crossfield Clo. TA6 3 D2
Crossview Rise. TA6 3 D1
Crowcombe Walk. TA6 3 C3
Crowpill La. TA6 4 B1
Crows La. TA6 5 F1
Dampiet St. TA6 4 B3
Danesboro Rd. TA6 3 D3
Davies Clo. A6 4 B6
Daws Clo. TA6 4 A6
Deacon Rd. TA6 5 E2
Deal Clo. TA6 5 F2
Devonshire St. TA6 4 D3
Dingley Clo. TA6 4 A3
Dorset Rd. TA6 5 E5
Downhall Dri. TA6 3 D2
Drakes Clo. TA6 4 B2
Duncombe Clo. TA6 5 F3
Dunkery Rd. TA6 3 D4
Dunwear La. TA6 5 E5
Durleigh Clo. TA6 3 D4
Durleigh Hill. TA5 3 B6
Durleigh Rd. TA6 3 B4
East Quay. TA6 4 C2
Eastern Av. TA6 5 F4
Eastover. TA6 4 C3
Eastwood Clo. TA6 5 E4
Edinburgh Rd. TA6 4 A6
Edward St. TA6 4 D3
Eldergrove Clo. TA6 5 F1
Elizabeth Way. TA6 5 E3
Elmgrove Clo. TA6 5 F1
Elmside Rd. TA6 4 A5
Elmwood Av. TA6 4 B5
Enmore Rd. TA5 3 A5
Evesham Dri. TA6 4 C6
Fairfax Clo. TA6 5 E2
Fairfax Rd. TA6 5 E2
Farthing Rd. TA6 4 B6
Fernleigh Av. TA6 4 C5
Feversham Av. TA6 4 A2
Firtree Clo. TA6 5 F3
Fore St. TA6 4 B3
Frampton Rd. TA6 4 B6
Frederick Rd. TA6 5 E2
Friarn Av. TA6 4 B4
Friarn St. TA6 4 B3
Furlongs Av. TA6 4 A5
Furze Clo. TA6 3 D4
George St. TA6 4 B3
Gloucester Rd. TA6 4 B6
Gooch Clo. TA6 4 D3
Gordon Ter. TA6 4 C3
Grange Dri. TA6 3 D4
Grassmere Clo. TA6 3 C2
Greatwood Clo. TA6 4 C6
Grebe Clo. TA6 4 D4
Grebe Rd. TA6 4 D4
Greenacre. TA6 3 D2
Hagget Clo. TA6 4 B6
Halesleigh Rd. TA6 4 A3
Halsway. TA6 5 E3
Halswell Clo. TA6 4 A4
Hamp Av. TA6 4 B5
Hamp Brook Way. TA6 4 A6
Hamp Green Rise. TA6 4 B5
Hamp St. TA6 4 B5
Hampton Clo. TA6 5 E1
Hawkridge Rd. TA6 3 C4
Hawthorn Clo. TA6 5 F4
Haygrove Rd. TA6 3 D4
Hazelwood Dri. TA6 5 F3
Heathcombe Rd. TA6 3 B3
Heather Clo. TA6 4 D5
High St. TA6 4 B3
Highgrove Clo. TA6 4 C6
Hillgrove Clo. TA6 4 A3
Holford Rd. TA6 3 B3
Hollow La. TA6 3 C1
Holly Clo. TA6 5 F3
Hornbeam Clo. TA6 5 F2
Horse Pond. TA6 4 B4
Hughes Clo. TA6 4 D3
INDUSTRIAL & RETAIL:
Blake Ind Pk. TA6 4 C4
Castlefield Business Pk. TA6 4 C1
Colley La Ind Est. TA6 4 D5
Inwood Rd. TA6 3 C2
Irene Clo. TA6 5 F1
Ivygrove Clo. TA6 5 F1
Janson Clo. TA6 5 F2
Japonica Clo. TA6 5 F2
Jubilee Clo. TA6 5 E3
Juniper Clo. TA6 5 F3
Keltings. TA6 3 C2
Kendale Rd. TA6 4 A2
Kensington Gdns. TA6 5 F2
Kent Av. TA6 4 C5
Kestrel Clo. TA6 5 E4
Kidsbury Rd. TA6 4 A2
Kimberley Ter. TA6 4 D2
King George Av. TA6 4 B5
King Sq. TA6 4 B3
King St. TA6 4 C3
Kingfisher Clo. TA6 5 E5
Kings Pl. TA6 4 B3
Knightsbridge Way. TA6 5 F2
Knowle Rd. TA6 5 E1
Laburnum Clo. TA6 5 F4
Ladymead Clo. TA6 3 B4
Lamb La. TA6 4 B3
Larch Clo. TA6 5 F2
Leeward Clo. TA6 5 E4
Leyton Dri. TA6 5 F2
Liberty Pl. TA6 4 D4
Limetree Clo. TA6 5 F3
Linden Clo. TA6 5 E4
Linham Rd. TA6 4 B2
Linley Clo. TA6 5 F1
Longacre Dro. TA7 5 H3
Longstone Av. TA6 5 E4
Lower Bath Rd. TA6 4 D2
Loxleigh Av. TA6 4 D4
Ludlow Clo. TA6 4 C6
Luxborough Rd. TA6 3 B4
Lyndale Av. TA6 4 A3
Lyndhurst Cres. TA6 3 C3
Magnolia Tree Clo. TA6 5 F3
Mallard Way. TA6 4 C4
Malvern Clo. TA6 5 F2
Mandarin Clo. TA6 4 D4
Manor Rd. TA6 5 E2
Mansion Ho La. TA6 4 B3
Market St. TA6 4 B3
Marlborough Av. TA6 4 C6
Marlborough Clo. TA6 4 C6
Mayfield Dri. TA6 3 B4
Mayflower Clo. TA6 5 F3
Mead Ct. TA6 4 A5
Meadow Park. TA6 3 C3
Mendip Rd. TA6 5 E3
Merle Clo. TA6 4 D4
Merridge Clo. TA6 3 B4
Middle Stream Clo. TA6 4 A6
Millwood Clo. TA6 4 A6
Milne Clo. TA6 4 B6
Milton Pl. TA6 4 A4
Monmouth St. TA6 4 C3
Moores La. TA6 3 B1
Moorland Rd. TA6 5 E4
Moorland Way. TA6 5 F3
Moots La. TA6 5 E4
Moss Clo. TA6 5 E2
Mount St. TA6 4 B3
Mulberry Tree Clo. TA6 5 F3
Myrtle Clo. TA6 5 F2
Nelson Ct. TA6 4 B2
New Rd. TA6 4 C3
New Rd. TA5 3 A1
Nicholls Clo. TA6 3 D4
Nightingale Clo. TA6 5 E4
Norfolk Clo. TA6 5 E5
North St. TA6 4 A3
Northfield. TA6 4 A4
Northgate. TA6 4 B2
Nursery Ter. TA6 4 A3
Oakfield Rd. TA6 3 C4
Oakgrove Way. TA6 5 F1
Old Taunton Rd. TA6 4 C4
Orchard La. TA6 3 D3
Osborne Rd. TA6 4 B2
Palmer Clo. TA6 4 B6
Palmtree Clo. TA6 5 F3
Park Av. TA6 3 D4
Park Rd. TA6 4 A4
Park Wall Dro. TA7 5 H1
Park Way. TA6 5 E1
Parkstone Av. TA6 4 C5
Parrett Way. TA6 4 D4
Peace Clo. TA6 5 F2
*Peachtree Clo, Tulip Tree Rd. TA6 5 F2
Pear Tree Clo. TA6 5 F4
Pelham Ct. TA6 5 F1
Pembroke Rd. TA6 5 E5
Penarth Rd. TA6 3 D3
Penelorlieu. TA6 4 B3
Penlea Av. TA6 4 A5
Penlea Clo. TA6 4 A6
Penzoy Av. TA6 4 D4
Petrel Clo. TA6 5 F1
Phillips Clo. TA6 3 D4
Phoenix Rd. TA6 4 D4
Pine Tree Clo. TA6 5 F3
Plum La. TA6 5 E6
Plum Tree Clo. TA6 5 F3
Polden St. TA6 4 C3
Pollard Rd. TA6 5 F2
Popham Clo. TA6 5 F2
Poplar Rd. TA6 5 F1
Portland Pl. TA6 3 D3
Portwall Dro. TA7 5 H3
Potterton Clo. TA6 4 B6
Priory Ct. TA6 4 B3
Provident Pl. TA6 4 A3
Purley Dri. TA6 5 F1
Pyrland Walk. TA6 3 B3
Quantock Av. TA6 3 D3
Quantock Meadow. TA6 3 C3
Quantock Rd. TA6 3 A1
Quantock Ter. TA6 4 C2
Quantock Way. TA6 3 C3
Quayside. TA6 4 B2
Queen St. TA6 4 B3
Queens Rd. TA6 4 B6
Queenswood Rd. TA6 3 C4
Raglan Clo. TA6 5 E1
Raleigh Clo. TA6 5 E3
Redgate St. TA6 4 D3
Reed Clo. TA6 4 B6
Regent Way. TA6 4 C6
Rhode La. TA6 4 A6
Ringwood Rd. TA6 4 C6
Risedale Clo. TA6 3 C2
Risemoor Rd. TA6 4 A6
River View Ter. TA6 4 B2
Robert Dri. TA6 4 C5
Robins Dri. TA6 4 C2
Roe Clo. TA6 5 E4
Roman La. TA6 3 C4
Rope Walk. TA6 4 C3
Rosary Dri. TA6 3 B4
Rosebery Av. TA6 4 D2
Rosevean Clo. TA6 5 F1
Rowans Clo. TA6 5 E2
Ruborough Rd. TA6 5 E4
Ruggs Dro. TA7 5 H6
Russell Pl. TA6 4 B2
St Davids Ct. TA6 5 F4
St James Ct. TA6 5 F4
St John St. TA6 4 C3
St Marks Ct. TA6 5 F5
St Mary St. TA6 4 B3
St Matthews Field. TA6 4 A4
St Matthews Grn. TA6 4 A4
St Pauls Ct. TA6 5 F5
St Peters Ct. TA6 5 F4
St Saviours Av. TA6 4 C4
St Thomas Ct. TA6 5 F5
Salmon Par. TA6 4 C3
Saltlands. TA6 4 B1
Saltlands Av. TA6 4 B1
Sandford Hill. TA5 3 A1
Sandown Clo. TA6 4 C6
Sandpiper Clo. TA6 4 C4
Sandpiper Rd. TA6 4 C4
Sandringham Clo. TA6 5 E1
Saxon Grn. TA6 5 E3
Saxon Rd. TA6 5 E4
Seaward Dri. TA6 4 B2
Sedge Clo. TA6 4 B6
Sedgemoor Rd. TA6 4 D5
Selworthy Clo. TA6 4 B6
Severn Clo. TA6 5 F1
Seymour Rd. TA6 5 F3
Shearwater Clo. TA6 5 E4
Shellthorn Gro. TA6 4 B6
Shepherds Clo. TA6 3 D2
Sheridan Clo. TA6 5 F5
Shervage Ct. TA6 5 E3
Silver St. TA6 4 B3
Silverdale Clo. TA6 3 C2
Skimmerton La. TA5 3 A2
Somerset Gdns. TA6 5 E4
Somerset Rd. TA6 5 E4
Somerton Clo. TA6 5 F4
Somerville Way. TA6 5 F5
Southgate Av. TA6 4 C5
Sovereign Rd. TA6 5 F1
Spaxton Rd. TA5 3 A2
Spencer Clo. TA6 5 F5
Spillers Clo. TA6 4 A6
Spoonbill Rd. TA6 4 D4
Springfield Av. TA6 3 D5
Springley Rd. TA6 5 F2
Squibbs Clo. TA6 5 F2
Stafford Rd. TA6 5 E5
Stanley Clo. TA6 4 B6
Stockmoor Clo. TA6 4 C6
Stratton Clo. TA6 5 E5
Suffolk Clo. TA6 5 E5
Sully Clo. TA6 5 F2
Summerway Drove. TA7 5 G4
Sunnybank Rd. TA6 4 A5
Sunnymead. TA6 4 A5
Sussex Av. TA6 4 D5
Sussex Clo. TA6 4 D4
Sycamore Clo. TA6 5 F3
Sydenham Clo. TA6 5 E2
Sydenham Rd. TA6 5 E1
Symons Way. TA6 4 C1
Taunton Rd. TA6 4 C4
Taylor Ct. TA6 4 C3
Teak Clo. TA6 5 F2
Teal Clo. TA6 4 C4
Temblett Grn. TA6 3 D3
Tetton Clo. TA6 3 B3
The Clink. TA6 4 C2
The Copse. TA6 5 F3
The Drove. TA6 4 C1
The Green. TA6 4 A5
The Laurels. TA6 3 D2
The Leggar. TA6 4 C2
The Oaks. TA6 3 D2
The Pippins. TA6 3 D2
Thompson Clo. TA6 5 F2
Thorncombe Cres. TA6 5 E2
Timberscombe Way. TA6 3 B4
Tone Dri. TA6 4 D5
Town Bridge. TA6 4 C3
Trevor Rd. TA6 5 E1
Trinity Ct. TA6 4 B2
Triscombe. TA6 3 D4
Tudor Way. TA6 4 C6
Tulip Tree Rd. TA6 5 F3
Turner Clo. TA6 4 C4
Tynte Rd. TA6 5 F2
Union St. TA6 4 D2
Valetta Pl. TA6 4 B2
Vicars La. TA6 3 D3
Victoria Rd. TA6 4 A3
Wadham Clo. TA6 5 F2
Walnut Dri. TA6 5 E4
Walton Clo. TA6 5 F3
Wares La. TA6 3 D2
Warren Clo. TA6 4 B1
Warwick Av. TA6 5 E5
Washington Gdns. TA6 4 A3
Waterford Clo. TA6 4 C6
Watsons La. TA6 4 C3
Waverley Rd. TA6 4 B2
Weacombe Rd. TA6 5 E2
Wellington Rd. TA6 4 D3
Wembdon Hill. TA6 3 B1
Wembdon Rise. TA6 3 D2
Wembdon Rd. TA6 4 A3
Wessex Clo. TA6 5 E4
West Quay. TA6 4 C3
West St. TA6 4 A4
Westercombe Clo. TA6 3 B3
Western Way. TA6 4 B1
Westfield Clo. TA6 4 B4
Westonzoyland Rd. TA6 4 D4
Westover Grn. TA6 4 A4
Westwood Rd. TA6 5 F1
Whitebeam Clo. TA6 5 F2
Whites Clo. TA6 4 B6
Whitfield Rd. TA6 5 F1
Wilkins Rd. TA6 5 F3
Willoughby Rd. TA6 3 C4
Willow Ct. TA6 5 F3
Willow Walk. TA6 5 E4
Wills Rd. TA6 4 A6
Wind Down Clo. TA6 3 C3
Windsor Rd. TA6 5 E1
Witches Walk. TA6 4 A6
Withygrove Clo. TA6 5 F1
Wolmer Clo. TA6 4 B6
Woodbury Rd. TA6 3 D3
Wordsworth Av. TA6 4 B2
Wrenmoor Clo. TA6 5 E5
Wye Av. TA6 5 E4
Wylds Rd. TA6 4 C1
Wyndham Rd. TA6 5 E2
Yeo La. TA6 4 D5
Yeo Rd. TA6 4 D5
York Bldgs. TA6 4 B3
York Rd. TA6 4 B6

NORTH PETHERTON

Alder Clo. TA6 6 C6
Balls La. TA6 6 A4
Baymead Clo. TA6 6 C4
Baymead La. TA6 6 C5
Baymead Meadow. TA6 6 C5
Beggs Clo. TA6 6 C5
Binding Clo. TA6 6 C4
Blackthorn Clo. TA6 6 C6
Bridgwater Rd. TA6 6 C4
Broadlands Av. TA6 6 C5
Brook Clo. TA6 6 A5
Butts Corner. TA6 6 C4
Canns La. TA6 6 C4
Chaucer Clo. TA6 6 C4
Clare St. TA6 6 B4
Clarence Dri. TA6 6 B4
Cliff Rd. TA6 6 A5
Crosswell Clo. TA6 6 B5
Dancing Hill. TA6 6 A4
Dyers Grn. TA6 6 B5
Ellen Clo. TA6 6 C4
Fore St. TA6 6 B5
Hammet St. TA6 6 B5
Hardings Clo. TA6 6 C5
Heathfield Clo. TA6 6 C4
High St. TA6 6 B5
Holly Clo. TA6 6 C6
Hulkshay La. TA6 6 A5
Hyde Pk. TA6 6 B5
Hyde Pk Av. TA6 6 B5
Ivors Way. TA6 6 B4
King Alfred Clo. TA6 6 C4
Lindsey Cres. TA6 6 C5
McCreath Clo. TA6 6 C5
Maple Clo. TA6 6 C6
Meade Clo. TA6 6 C5
Melcombe La. TA6 6 A5
Milestone Clo. TA6 6 C4
Mill St. TA6 6 B5
Newton Rd. TA6 6 B5
North St. TA6 6 B4
Old Rd. TA6 6 C4
Orchard Clo. TA6 6 B5
Parkfield Clo. TA6 6 C4
Pilots Helm. TA6 6 B4
Portman Cres. TA6 6 B6
Portman Dri. TA6 6 B6
Portman Rd. TA6 6 B6
Princess Clo. TA6 6 C4
Quantock Clo. TA6 6 B4
Queen St. TA6 6 B4
Rectory Clo. TA6 6 B5
Rogers Clo. TA6 6 C5
St Marys Cres. TA6 6 C4
School Fields. TA6 6 C5
School La. TA6 6 C5
Shovel La. TA6 6 B6
Sunnybrow Clo. TA6 6 C4
Tappers La. TA6 6 B5
Taunton Rd. TA6 6 B6
Verriers. TA6 6 B5
Watery La. TA6 6 B4
Whiting La. TA6 6 B5

PURITON

Batch Rd. TA7 6 D1
Birch Av. TA7 6 D2
Bristol Rd. TA6 6 A1
Canns La. TA7 6 D1
Church Field La. TA7 6 C1
Court Gro. TA7 6 D1
Cypress Dri. TA7 6 D2
Downend Cres. TA6 6 A2
Downend Rd. TA6 6 A2
Downend Ter. TA6 6 B2
Dunball Dro. TA6 6 A2
Hall Rd. TA7 6 C2
Hill Side. TA7 6 D2
Hillside Cres. TA7 6 D2
Hillside Dri. TA7 6 D2
Manse La. TA7 6 D2
Maple Clo. TA7 6 D2
Middle St. TA7 6 D1
Newlyn Cres. TA7 6 C1
Northmead Drove. TA7 6 D1
Parsonage Ct. TA7 6 C1
Pawlett Rd. TA6 6 B1
Pool Clo. TA7 6 D1
Purewell. TA7 6 D1
Puriton Hill. TA7 6 C2
Puriton Park. TA7 6 D2
Riverton Rd. TA7 6 C2
Rookery Clo. TA7 6 D1
Rowan Clo. TA7 6 D2
Rowlands Rise. TA7 6 C2
Rye. TA7 6 C1
Station Rd. TA6 6 B3
Tatinee Ct. TA7 6 D1
Walnut Clo. TA7 6 D2
Waterloo. TA7 6 D1
Waterloo Clo. TA7 6 D1
Webbers Way. TA7 6 C2
Woolavington Rd. TA7 6 C2

Edition 418 F 2.02.